THE T'AI CHI WORKBOOK

Paul Crompton

THE T'AI CHI WORKBOOK

SHAMBHALA/Boston
1987

SHAMBHALA PUBLICATIONS, INC.
Horticultural Hall
300 Massachusetts Avenue
Boston, Massachusetts 02115

© 1986 by Paul Crompton

Printed in the United States of America
Distributed in the United States by Random House

LIBRARY OF CONGRESS CATALOGING-IN-PUBLICATION DATA

Crompton, Paul
    The T'ai Chi workbook.

    Includes index.
    1. T'ai chi ch'üan. I. Title.
CV504.C76   1987   796.8'155   87-9736
ISBN 0-87773-424-0 (pbk.)

Photographs in Chapter 7 by Lou Ann Richards
All other photographs by Eamonn McCabe

To Bridget
Who went through it all with me

CONTENTS

		Page
	Introduction	ix
1	Approach	1
2	Experiences of T'ai Chi as Student and Teacher	7
3	Relaxation — Key to 'Chi' of T'ai Chi	18
4	Form and Meaning	36
5	Push Hands Training	90
6	T'ai Chi for Self Defence	106
7	T'ai Chi and Other Arts	123
8	T'ai Chi for Health and Sanity	131
9	The 'Chi' of T'ai Chi	138
10	Additional Relaxation Methods	146
11	Review	148
12	Some Background to the Art	150
	Index	157

INTRODUCTION

T'ai Chi Chuan is one of the great Chinese gifts to mankind. In different forms it has survived the wars and catastrophes which have befallen its country of origin, and today flourishes in most parts of the world. Perhaps its survival is due to its gentle nature; it is not hard but soft and flowing, like the Tao, life itself.

In this book I have tried to offer to you a broad picture of the art of T'ai Chi Chuan, a methodical way into its practical study, and some of my own experiences, thoughts and feelings. As I am English and not Chinese, I hope that my exposition will do more to open the subject to Western students than most of the books written by Chinese authors. The latter's works mainly take the form of a step-by-step description of what to do, but not how to do it, not how to 'get into it'.

If you follow what I say and apply it then your journey into T'ai Chi Chuan will be one of discovery. Your study will be well founded, and you will have found a friend for life — yourself!

1 APPROACH

I first came across T'ai Chi Chuan in 1967. Mrs Gerda Geddes, a well-known figure in T'ai Chi circles, gave a demonstration of the art to some people who were interested in the Alexander system of postural re-education. She had returned after some years in Hong Kong and I think that hers was one of the first public performances. Everyone was impressed and captivated by her movements. They were beautiful, co-ordinated, and full of effortless control. I decided that I had to find out more. With the passage of time, as I studied the art myself, I realised that there was more to it than the aesthetic satisfaction of my first impressions.

This passage of time to which I refer stretched from 1967 to 1984, and during this period I read dozens of books and magazine articles, studied with six different teachers, compared notes with many other students and teachers and found that my appreciation of T'ai Chi Chuan was modified. Sometimes this modification came about gradually; at other times with a sudden leap. (From now on I will refer to our subject as T'ai Chi, leaving out the Chuan, since this is the commonly accepted abbreviation.)

Why Another Book?
Since there are quite a number of books in print on T'ai Chi you might well ask me why I am writing this one. There is a simple answer. It is that there is no book available which really takes pains to tell the reader how to get into the art. There are books which give a step-by-step guide to the movements – this is not enough – and there are books which discuss the relationship between T'ai Chi and different aspects of Chinese philosophy and art; but not one I know of which shows that the author is really trying to *share* his experience with the reader, for their mutual benefit. It is rather like some books about how to look after your car. There are plenty of manuals on specific cars, how they work, how to service and how to repair one. But everyone knows that when you come to try and service your car then you run into difficulties which somehow were never mentioned in the service manual.

In this book I am trying to foresee the difficulties and questions you may encounter in studying T'ai Chi, as well as show you how to do it, and by referring to my own experience suggesting how you go about solving and answering them. A book is not a living teacher, but a book is always there, to be referred to. By emphasising certain principles, over and over as the book progresses, I hope that by the time you have absorbed it your approach to the art will be well founded. Then, if you learn with a teacher as well, whoever he or she is, English, Chinese, American or Japanese, you will be in a good position to grasp what he is trying to convey to you.

Oriental Brevity

Let me give an example of what I mean about learning. A characteristic of oriental teaching methods is their brevity. Where we in the West are apt to give long explanations, analyses and expositions to put over our points, a Chinese is often not so inclined. Maybe he is just saving his energy, but whatever the reason when he is teaching you T'ai Chi he may say, 'When you do this movement, keep your elbows down.'

He will not add anything else. Why you should keep your elbows down, what part this plays in the overall system of movement, how it relates to the anatomy and physiology of the body, and so on, are not mentioned.

There are several reasons for this. One is that traditionally the Chinese are very secretive about what they know. A Chinese friend of mine, aged about 55, kept the fact that he had studied Kung fu secret from his brother-in-law until he was well into middle-age. It is traditional to do this, to keep knowledge secret within the blood-related members of the family, so that outsiders cannot benefit. Another reason is that a student, if he were given just a little knowledge, would have to struggle and make efforts to show that he was worthy of more. In this way too he would also become more able to study for himself. He would take the brief statements of his teacher and marry them to his experience.

This is an excellent method, but in my experience it does not work with Western students. Western education has so conditioned most of us that we are on the whole unable to carry out this task of relating new knowledge to what we already know unless we receive plenty of this new knowledge. And it has to be repeated and repeated. We are programmed to memorise, rather than to dig for new relationships on the basis of a few short sentences. My own experience shows me that if you tell a student to keep his feet shoulder width apart, and then expect him to remember and apply this instruction, and understand why, you are going to be disappointed.

T'ai Chi may be Chinese Soft Exercise but inside the soft is the iron, as you will discover as you study.

So, I will try to explain as clearly as I can in the space available exactly why you do the things you do in T'ai Chi. I will show you ways of experiencing them, and then you will find the firm foundation which I spoke about. You will find what is fundamental.

What Is 'Fundamental'?

Yes, what is fundamental to T'ai Chi? It is fundamental to T'ai Chi to do as little as possible to achieve your goal. This does not mean that we try to become lazy or skip training; nothing like that. In fact we are not going to be able to make clear what we do mean by doing as little as possible in the introductory chapter. I just put the question to you now, that if I asked you to get up from the chair

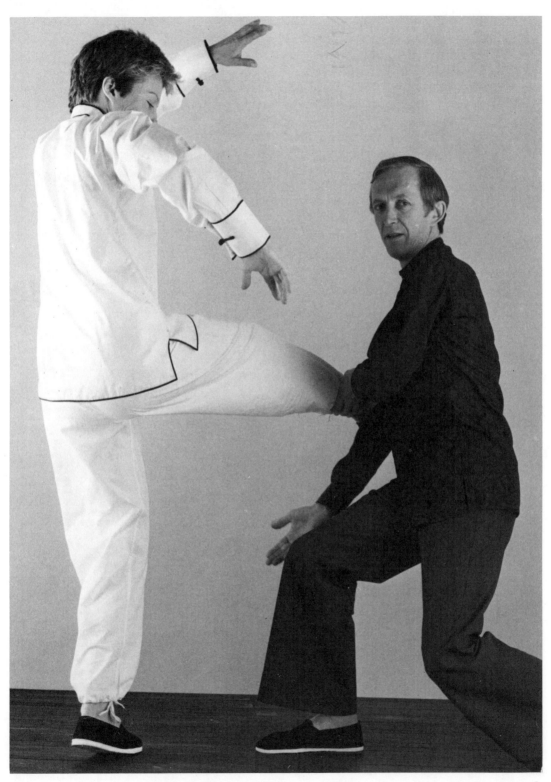

4

where you are sitting to read this book and go and make a cup of coffee, but to do as little as possible to make it; how would you do it? If you know already then you are a master of T'ai Chi. If you don't, then read on. In fact, don't read on. Just go and make a cup of tea or coffee, whichever you prefer, and do as little as possible in every sense.

Did you enjoy it? Good. So, the last few paragraphs have been about why the book has been written: expanding the traditional Chinese brevity and exploring the meaning of 'fundamental'. Can I hear you saying that the author of this book is a big head and that you can grasp brevity and fundamentals just as well as he can? Well, you are wrong, because I too failed to understand the brief statements of my teachers and I am still trying to put the fundamentals into my daily training.

The 'Secrets'

This book will also cover some of the classical teachings, give autobiographical experiences and outline the vague history of T'ai Chi into this century when documented facts took the place of rumour and legend.

'One dog barks at a shadow and the rest bark at the sound....'

A final point is worth making here. The East is a mysterious region for us in the West, even today. This fact plays strongly on the feelings and imagination of some students, and is often taken advantage of by some teachers of T'ai Chi. Students frequently come to classes looking for mystery. They want to be initiated into secrets which the master, seen always as a sage-like figure, will gradually reveal to them from the innermost depths of his wisdom. This may put the teacher and the student in false positions. The student is giving vent to his imagination, to the entire detriment of his common sense, intelligence and progress in training; and the teacher is being cast in a role which he is often unable to put aside.

This leads to a situation in which the student is always looking for the next thing which he may be told, for some mystery to be revealed, and the teacher is constantly giving it to him in the form of pithy statements and wise sounding innuendoes. From such a state of affairs the student is always looking into the future, instead of applying himself to what is in front of his nose. Thus, we have a parody of the real situation which potentially exists. There are 'mysteries' but they are all practical ones. They must be approached in a practical way.

I lay some of the blame for mistaken approaches to T'ai Chi on the marvellous book of Taoist wisdom, the *Tao Te Ching*. Not on the book itself but on the way a lot of people take it. It is possible to become intoxicated, mesmerised, transported by this book, but that is all in the mind, it is not absorbed by the body. Many people have approached T'ai Chi and performed it, in this state of Tao-Te-

Ching-intoxication. They overlook the practical requirements of the body. It is the teacher's job to teach these practicalities. From these practicalities will come the miracle of new experience, real experience, which is indeed itself a mystery, since so few of us ever have it. From this experience a new relationship with the sayings of the *Tao Te Ching* can come.

First read each chapter carefully. If you can restrain yourself, which I never could, do not try to do any of the exercises and movements until you have finished the whole book. Then, before you begin to move, make sure that you mentally grasp what you are going to try. Let your body follow what you know. If you do not do this you will get habits which later you will find hard to break.

2 EXPERIENCES OF T'AI CHI
AS STUDENT AND TEACHER

When I began to study T'ai Chi I had been training in martial arts and other oriental studies for a long time. Consequently, I had learned how to approach this new subject with what is traditionally considered to be a 'right' attitude. This means for instance that it is right for the student to have respect for his teacher, not to criticise what he is teaching, not to think that he, the student, knows better than his teacher, and to pay attention to what he is being taught, not to forget it, and to train with diligence in between lessons so that the teacher does not have to keep going over the same material time and time again, thus taxing his own patience and possibly wasting the time of other members of the class.

However, a possible accompaniment to this uncritical approach can be that both student and teacher develop an attitude that theirs is the only way of doing something, be it T'ai Chi, swordplay, Karate, or whatever. On a higher level than this, a teacher recognises that his is not the only way, it is 'his' way. Unfortunately, as I discovered, the attitude of live and let live is not the most prevalent and many do criticise others and attempt to undermine their reputations, frequently without any justification — a shortsighted approach. However, I was unaware of all this at the beginning and my own attitude as I have said reflected the traditional one.

The effect of such an attitude of respect is of benefit to the student, in this case myself, because it mobilises the attention. If I had not been respectful and mindful of what my teacher was saying and doing, if I had half listened, gazed out of the window, shuffled my feet and scratched my head, I would not have remembered what he was conveying. As it was, I listened and repeated his every T'ai Chi move, and when he had gone I went over and over what had happened during the one-hour lesson.

Learn Slowly
Not only is T'ai Chi performed slowly but it is learned slowly. That is to say, most students cannot learn more than one or two postures at a time. For some reason, perhaps our cerebrally oriented education, Western people absorb T'ai Chi very slowly. They need time to get used to the new way of moving, not only at the beginning of their study but all the way through it. Only very gradually do they become able to learn the postures and the form a little more quickly. Of course, with the right attitude I was speaking of, it is not important to hurry, but many people chafe at this and want to get on to the next posture and the next, without first accurately performing the current one. Another way of expressing this is to say that they want to change *and* remain the same. They study T'ai Chi for some reason which implies change but they find it hard to

accept the means. There are no pills which will transform the beginner into a competent T'ai Chi practitioner overnight. But that is not our Western attitude — we are pill prone people.

My first teacher was from New York. He had studied with an excellent and respected Chinese for some years and his approach was to teach me a few postures at a time. He was also a musician who had been featured on records playing oriental music and this came out in the sensitivity of his T'ai Chi presentation. In turn I picked up some of this and it helped me. I also picked up some of his mannerisms, which did not. His insistence on accuracy and correct Form in moving was very marked, and he did not let errors pass unnoticed.

An important point which only occurred to me after some months should be mentioned here. He and I were not the same! He was taller, bigger boned and with a much longer body. He was a different nationality and had a different outlook on life in general. He was married with no children; I was married with children. Consequently, many factors contributed to our differences in approach and moving. So, when you begin to study T'ai Chi, bear the differences as well as the similarities of interest in mind. Do not imagine that you can or even should emulate your teacher in every way.

Another of my teachers was a large, rolling, big bodied man. I am thin and light. There is no way I can do T'ai Chi the same; we are opposites. I have to find my own way. So we can say that it is the principles of T'ai Chi which are important, and as long as these are adhered to the differences in build and physique are unimportant. This applies to psychological differences as well.

Some people learn in a different way from others. Some respond to directional diagrams such as north, south, east, west, mentioned later in this book. Others have no connection with diagrammatic explanations and need mainly to see what to do. Others 'feel' what is being shown to them in a T'ai Chi class, and this is their starting point. Most people of course learn from a combination of these methods and I was no exception. I found the four cardinal points of the compass and their sub-divisions useful in learning the Form or sequence of movements, I was also aware of the way my teachers moved, and had some experience of paying attention to new movements through my earlier training. Consequently, when I was alone I could draw on all these sources to help me remember and reproduce what I had learned. You yourself may find other ways as well as these.

Not Traditional
In the East it is not traditional in T'ai Chi for a teacher to go over and over a lesson using verbal explanations. The emphasis is placed on watching how the teacher performs his actions and then reproducing them to the best of one's ability. I found, when I

began teaching T'ai Chi myself, that 90 per cent of Western students, and a few Chinese who came to my classes, were not able to do this. Their attention in this field was too weak for them to communicate to their bodies what their eyes had seen. But this ability can be strengthened, like a muscle, and I sometimes advised students to watch cats, or other animals, or other people, and see if they could move in a similar way, thus exercising their ability. I also devised stretching exercises or used others which I had learned, such as the Surya Namaskars of India, to widen their experience of movement. The intention was to get them 'into their bodies'.

Gradually, I moved through my study of the Long Form, learning the poetic names of such postures as White Crane Spreads Wings, and White Snake Puts out Toungue, Step Back to Drive the Monkey Away and Wave Hands in the Clouds. I was intrigued and wooed by this strange new way of moving; passionately wishing to learn every single thing that I could. I trained constantly, sometimes straining the patience of my wife who would come into the living room or garden to find chairs moved back or flower pots re-arranged and a general air of inconvenience pervading our home.

Then I began to experience the transient feeling of peace and calm whilst doing the Long Form which is characteristic of T'ai Chi. This is only possible once at least a few of the movements have been learned, once the body itself is sure of what to do, and is acclimatised to the new atmosphere. Whilst the brain is engaged in learning, the body is not free to move and the brain to remain awake and alert without being pestered by thoughts of what to do next. T'ai Chi has been called 'meditation in movement' and at its highest level it is just that. There was once a BBC television series called 'The Long Search' which showed in one of its episodes a Buddhist monk in a remote part of Ceylon. He was doing a form of walking meditation which consisted of stepping very slowly back and forth along the same track, and doing it in such a way that every movement was co-ordinated, every breath in time and harmony with his body, every turn made without a break in the gentle flow. In a word, he was a T'ai Chi master though he had probably never heard of the art.

When one sees such a sight, which is rare of course, one is tempted to imagine that one can do the same. But even to attempt this kind of discipline without preparation is a mistake in my opinion. This man's harmony came from deep within. His harmonious breathing, in tune with his inner state, had not been regulated by imagination or some instruction from his mind. One movement comes from within, and the other comes from the outside, from imitation. To approach it one needs a teacher. What I used to teach my own students was that when they were performing the movements correctly their breath might change naturally of its own accord, just as a man who has been walking or digging for a long time will find that his body has itself adjusted its breathing.

9

There is no rational justification for trying to 'teach' the body how to breathe.

Another aspect of this peaceful state which I mentioned is that I found I was much more aware of the air around me. When we move in our usual way we are not sensitive to the air, not to the smell of the air but the presence of the air. We are like fish who do not know of the existence of water. Because we are in it we do not feel it, we do not recognise its life-giving qualities nor the movement of our bodies through it. We are dead to it, asleep to it. T'ai Chi study is one of the ways to become more aware of this. I would begin to move so that I was 'swimming' through the air, 'floating' in the air, parting the air like water. Of course there is always the danger that a person can be carried away by such fanciful notions, but then it is time to come back to earth, check your posture, check your alignment, direction and so forth, and come down out of the clouds...

Gradually I was finding my way through the world of T'ai Chi until I came across the next step: Pushing Hands. As I learned very little about Pushing Hands from my first teacher I will discuss it later on, except to say that I began to realise when making contact with my teacher, in the way that T'ai Chi students are taught, how tense I was *vis-à-vis* another person. It is all very well to move in a relaxed, slow and gentle way alone, solo, but once another person puts some pressure on you, however light, then your entire condition changes.

After about eighteen months my teacher became involved with other classes and I could not learn from him. He was teaching the Royal Shakespeare Company and many people were taking up his time. I found myself alone, but with plenty to work on.

Then some friends who studied the Japanese art of Aikido told me about a woman, from China, who worked with the Hong Kong Bank in London. She was interested in Aikido but knew T'ai Chi well. She had learned from her father. I arranged to meet her, unaware that I was in for my first big shock.

I went to the club where she was learning her Aikido. When she had finished training my friends introduced us and partly as a result of this introduction and partly I could see out of curiosity she asked to see my T'ai Chi performance. I use the word 'curiosity' because in those days, the early 1970s, T'ai Chi was still virtually unknown in the West. Any Chinese person who met a westerner who claimed to be able to do it was bound to be interested. Even as late as 1981 when I met the official Wushu delegation from China in London, Chu Fenglian, a woman martial artist who was in the entourage, was surprised that I could perform T'ai Chi. Well, the Chinese woman watched me perform my movements at the Aikido club. When I came to the end of the first section I stopped and looked at her.

She shook her head. We began to talk and it emerged that she considered that I had learned entirely incorrectly. I was flabber-gasted, to say the least, but listened to what she had to say. She showed me the beginning of her own Form. Though recognisable as T'ai Chi to me, it was very different. She performed it with such precision and grace though that I immediately asked her to teach me. She agreed, on the spot, and I began my first lesson.

I discovered straight away that one of the chief differences between what she did and the T'ai Chi I had learned was in the position of the trunk. She rhythmically inclined forward and back into an upright posture with each new movement. As the T'ai Chi classics say that the spine must be kept vertical, it appeared that she was going contrary to that rule. But if the rule was interpreted that the spine be kept in a straight line then her inclination was acceptable. I did not question her about it at the time and was content to learn.

I went away and decided that whilst my new teacher was available I would suspend most of my study of the T'ai Chi I had learned and absorb this new Form. From then on I seized every opportunity to visit her and learn. She said very little when we met. Each time, she showed me a few moves, and I had to be observant enough to pick up what she was doing. She made me go over and over what I had seen but said almost nothing. She did tell me that her father was a nerve specialist in Hong Kong, and that he taught the art to patients of his to speed their recovery. She wrote to her father about me and he invited me to visit him, but I never got the opportunity.

My relationship with my second teacher had many traditional sides to it. We never had any formal arrangement. We had no fixed time and I never knew where she would be. I would telephone and someone would tell me where she was. I would then drive to the place and almost literally 'collar' her; she would teach me a little more, and we would separate. I learned in her flat, at shows, at Aikido clubs, at my own house, anywhere and everywhere. I also learned the beginnings of 'yielding', another principle of T'ai Chi which says that we should never meet force with force. On this occasion we had been talking about this principle and I pushed her on the shoulder. My hand just slid off as she yielded, using her scapula action.

What struck me most about her was the precision of her move-ments. She was always exact, never wasting effort on extraneous action. She also showed me an unusual way of walking which was designed to help in the performance of the Form. I came across this in another teacher's class later, again slightly different.

I had begun my new study in the winter months and as the hot days of summer came upon us I found that T'ai Chi really made me sweat. My forearms even would be covered in moisture after only a few minutes, and I realised that this was caused as much by unnecessary tension as by the movements. This sweat reaction is common in all martial arts and is put down not only to the immense exertion seen in Karate, for instance, but in the unusual stress which comes from learning a combat art form.

The months were turning into a year. I was nearly through this new Long Form. I had not completely abandoned my old Form, nor written it off as my new teacher advised. I had studied T'ai Chi further, myself, going into books and magazines and talking to other people in the field. I learned that the style she was teaching me was the Wu or Ng form. Prior to meeting her I had thought that the style I was learning was the only one, the famous Yang style, which had descended from the Chen style. Everyone thought that the Chen had disappeared, but when the Chinese 'cultural revolution' died down the Chen style had been discovered by the authorities, alive and kicking in one of the provinces. Through more reading I learned of the Sun style, and derivatives of the Yang and Wu styles. In short, there are several styles of T'ai Chi but the best known and most widely done is the Yang. It was brought to the Western world by Cheng Man-Ch'ing, at least he is the best known teacher of it. Cheng died some years ago. I regret to say that my second teacher, for all her generosity, friendliness, skill and insight, was unable to recognise any other style but her own. When she later returned to Hong Kong I thanked her and returned to the Yang style.

Some years later I was given a copy of a book in English and Chinese. It was illustrated by photographs of a woman doing T'ai Chi. No, it was not my teacher but the style shown was the Wu, and it was exactly what I had been shown. It was published in Malaysia and gave me a strange thrill to recognise the movements so clearly from so far away.

I continued to study T'ai Chi on my own and even gave a short demonstration of what I knew at the Budokwai Judo club in South Kensington, probably the oldest in Europe. I did not think of opening a class myself at the time since I still considered myself to be a beginner, even though I 'knew' two Long Forms, Yang and Wu. Then, a Karate friend introduced me to a teacher of Pak Mei and Praying Mantis Kung fu. Briefly, I learned some of the movements from these styles but did not want to get involved in an entirely new way of moving. Both of these styles use a lot of explosive punching and grabbing techniques and are alien to T'ai Chi. What I did try was to take some of the Pak Mei and Mantis moves and perform them in a T'ai Chi manner, just to see what the experience would be like. Even then I found them out of keeping with T'ai Chi principles and put them aside for another day. However, the Pak Mei man had learned T'ai Chi in Hong Kong. Inevitably I showed him what I knew, and, inevitably now, he said that it was incorrect. As I had the very highest regard for his knowledge of Chinese martial arts I did not dispute what he said and watched as he showed me some of his own movements. His grace, smoothness and accuracy were marvellous to see. I was very impressed. But, he would not show me much. I had run into a hitherto unknown barrier — Chinese traditional secrecy. I would learn more of it in years to come, but I accepted his refusal and did not press him any further.

Some years had now passed since I first saw T'ai Chi for the first time. I was convinced that there is no such thing as 'correct' T'ai Chi; that only the principles should be held inviolate and the rest was merely a matter of what different human beings had made of them. I talked to other people and held my peace over any points of disagreement as I wished to learn as much as I possibly could.

Pushing Hands

Then I heard of a teacher new to England, from Taiwan, who was teaching Pushing Hands. I had had little experience of this training in which a pair of people in a pre-arranged way try to uproot or unbalance one another whilst trying to comply with the principles of the art. I have dealt with this in more detail elsewhere in the book. I went to this man's class and pretty soon I was learning how to use the press, push, roll-back, ward off, step, and so on, with a partner. I experienced the difficulty of remaining relaxed and the hard lesson of 'investing in loss', that is, being willing to suffer defeat or loss of balance in order to learn.

This teacher was as thin as the Pak Mei man was stout and when you tried to push him it was like trying to push a silk cloth hanging from a pole. There is no substance, no resistance, nothing solid. He was an expert in yielding and reminded me of the non-resisting Tao. As someone else put it to me when I discussed this man with him, 'There is no-body'. I had to agree — somehow there was no body. This teacher could disappear and still be there. He was like air; you push it but it just diffuses away in front of you. I learned a lot from him. I had some trying experiences but also made some happy discoveries such as a simple application of the movement called Fair Lady Works with Shuttle, during a session with a student from the USA.

Then, by invitation, I took my Pak Mei friend to see this man from Taiwan. The Pak Mei man was not very impressed. 'He is the teacher?' His voice was incredulous as he whispered the question to me. He behaved perfectly to the host and they spoke together for some time. The we watched the class and went away. My friend had come from a more 'sinewy' T'ai Chi background where the strength which can come from T'ai Chi was much more in evidence. Perhaps he did not take to the form the Taiwanese's softness assumed.

All these varied experiences confirmed in me the belief that T'ai Chi was wide open to interpretation. Whilst not wishing to abandon my respect for the fundamentals and spirit of the art, I had to admit that its practitioners were very divided in their views and

14

performance. My preoccupations with these questions were not empty, however, for the Pak Mei man went back to Hong Kong and studied more T'ai Chi with an elderly pupil of the famous Chen Wei Ming. When he came back he taught me unreservedly what he had learned. It was much more vigorous and demanding on the body. I duly tried it. The muscles of the body were exercised in a way that not many T'ai Chi students I have met ever experienced. Yet, and this was a significant 'yet', my friend did not teach me the Form he had originally learned from a student of one of the Yang family members at university in Hong Kong.

I did not press him. It would have needed a much deeper commitment than I was prepared to make in order for him to offer to teach me that Form. Also, my head was swimming with variations on variations of Forms. I took a rest from learning something new and concentrated on a little quiet digestion.

I did meet other students and teachers. In all, I can say that I had six main teachers of T'ai Chi up to the time of writing. For the present this is enough.

I can now move on to some entirely different episodes in my study of T'ai Chi, in which I tried to pass on to other people what I had learned. These were mainly young people, students, actors, singers and a few martial artists. This came about in two ways. There were few teachers on the subject in those days. I was constantly asked by those who knew me to show them how to do the Form, and in the end it seemed better to teach than to let them try to pick it up from the few books which were accurate and clear. I opened a small club and taught there once a week. Then through friends in the Alexander technique fraternity I was introduced to a class at the Royal Academy of Dramatic Art and to six classes at the Royal College of Music. The connection of T'ai Chi with the Alexander technique is one of correct posture and alignment, and my friends felt that the Chinese art would help students who were also pursuing training in the Alexander system.

When I began to teach I made plenty of mistakes, mostly ones of incorrect assumptions. One of these was that I believed that the students would be as interested in T'ai Chi as I was and would work as hard at it as I had. Of course they were not and did not. Secondly, they were very much concerned with 'expressing themselves' and using their bodies in an emotional way, which is not what T'ai Chi is basically about. However, I devised some methods to try to get around this.

One of the first things I discovered was how tense everyone is. You can do T'ai Chi whilst you are tense, but it is far from ideal. Secondly, many people feel embarrassed when asked to move in an entirely new way, especially if they have to do it in slow motion. The students would often begin to giggle, which broke

15

the concentration of others and so I had to find a way of dealing with or solving that. I made everyone lie down on the floor, before everything else, and we all told jokes, mainly Irish jokes, since they were the best known. Pretty soon everyone was laughing, even the people who did not want to laugh. When I judged that enough laughing had been going on, we all got up on our feet and did some loosening exercises, freeing the joints and bending and stretching in ways shown in this book. Only then did we turn to the movements of the Form.

Can't Remember?

A major problem of a different sort also became clear almost immediately. It is one which haunts many newcomers to T'ai Chi and at times brought me to a state of overwhelming amazement, since I had personally never had any difficulty with it. In most T'ai Chi postures your feet are placed shoulder width apart. This means that wherever your feet are − under you, behind you, in front of you − they do not stray beyond this fundamental distance, except in a few obvious and clearly understood cases. If you imagine that the distance between your shoulders is the distance between two parallel railway tracks, then whatever movement you make your feet are always on the lines or tracks. The feet do not go outside or inside the tracks. Look at the pictures to see what I mean.

 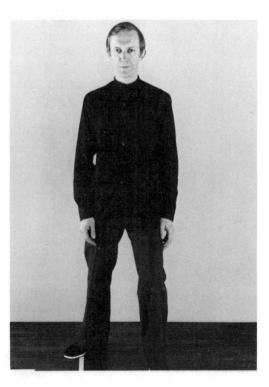

The reason for this is one of balance and relaxation. If your feet are closer together than your shoulder width your balance is not so good, and if they are further then you cannot move to the next posture as easily. I taught this fundamental distancing to the students in their first lesson, their second lesson and their third lesson. Many lessons later I was still teaching it. Some had picked it up and many had not. What could I do to help? I marked some parallel lines on the floor and asked them; can you keep your feet on those lines? This succeeded to some extent, and so if you have this difficulty yourself you could try this solution. The only problem with using it for fifteen different people is that they all have different distances between their shoulders.

From my own point of view, a difficulty I had was in relaxing my shoulders. When I used my arms my shoulders would invariably become too tense. It was only when one of my teachers taught me how to relax the scapula and its attendant muscles that I began to solve that one.

If you think about it, you will probably agree that you regard the bone and muscles at the top of your arm as your shoulder. It is your shoulder, of course, but it can best be truly relaxed by letting the scapula or shoulder blade descend naturally to its lowest level. When this happens the chest 'sinks' also. In the T'ai Chi classics it says 'sink the chest'. People try to sink their chests, by pressing down. The sinking of the chest follows from relaxing the scapula.

Put your left hand over your right shoulder. You will be touching a hard, horizontal ridge — the top of your scapula. Below it is a wad of muscles and a much thinner bone. This forms a rough triangle on your back, which moves over your back, that is, over your rib cage. The triangle is your scapula. Now, keeping your left hand lightly resting upon it, raise your right shoulder as high as you can. You will experience the muscle running along the top of your shoulder to your neck as it does the lifting. You will also be aware of the scapula as it rises.

Now let your shoulder fall. When it has fallen it will be at its lowest point, and the muscles which move it more able to relax. These muscles will not relax more unless you cultivate letting your scapula go down; do not pull it down, let it go down. This will help you in your T'ai Chi Form.

Let's move on to something practical for you to do.

3 RELAXATION — KEY TO 'CHI' OF T'AI CHI

Relaxation is the most important factor. The close partner of relax-ation is correct body alignment. The two go together like pepper and salt, gomasio and tamari, Adam and Eve. If you are really relaxed then your body will be correctly aligned, and if your body is correctly aligned you will be more relaxed. All the joints will be in the right relationship with one another. If they are not then there is strain, because one set of muscles is pulling harder than another, or the tone of the muscle is too strong or too weak. There is so much spoken about relaxation today, but not a lot of what is said is the relaxation we are looking for. A muscle can have an optimum tone; that is a quality of tension/relaxation balance which is just right. If the optimum tone is spread throughout the body then the 'chi' or vitality is not blocked and can circulate freely.

You may think that if you lie down you are relaxed, but this is scientifically proven to be untrue. Your subjective experience is wrong. Often when people lie down the small of the back is arched too far away from the ground. It is natural for a small arch to occur but in many of us it is too much because lumbar and sacral muscles are overly contracted.

If you lie down with your legs outstretched — see illustration — your lumbar region will arch. There is a natural arch at this point but not as much as most of us produce. Now put your feet flat on the floor. The arch should more or less disappear because of the new relation between legs and pelvis. If you still have a marked arch there then the lumbar region is too tense. In any case, you can use this position to give your spine an occasional rest. Note that when you take this position your muscles relax more. When you put your legs back out straight then there is a tightening up.

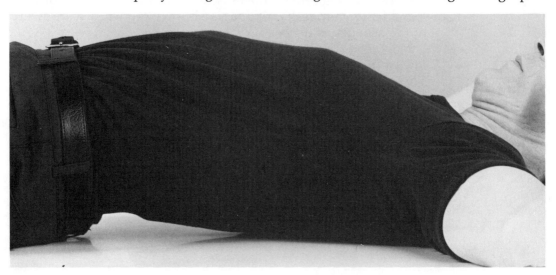

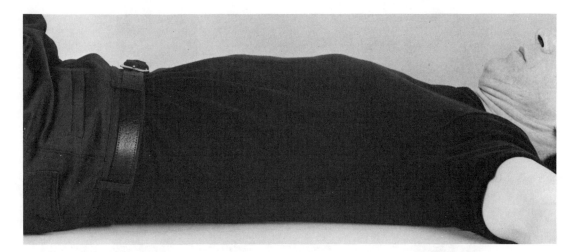

Look at the next illustration. You will see a person standing up in a T'ai Chi posture. Notice that his lumbar/sacral region is in the same line as that of the photograph showing the person with the feet flat on the floor. In the next illustration the person is once more bent too much, just as the position with the legs outstretched. In the case of the lying down photo it is to be expected, but in the standing one it is an adult postural defect. I say 'adult' because in a child it does not exist. Little children can even sit on the floor with a straight back.

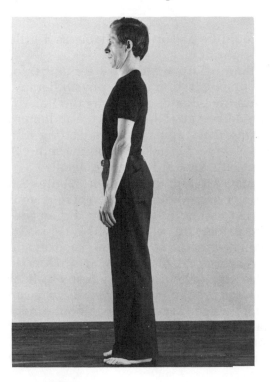

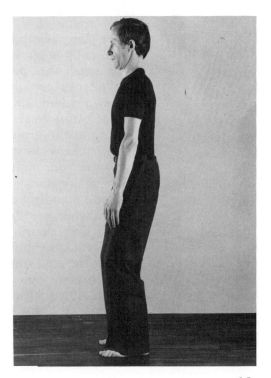

The Tao says that we should be as soft and pliable as a little child. Let's begin learning right now.

To reach this posture standing up we can try a number of methods: osteopathy, chiropractic, acupuncture, physiotherapy, rolfing, Feldenkrais and Alexander. But we can also try the T'ai Chi way of letting go at the knees, letting go at the feet, at the abdomen, folding at the groins, relaxing the scapula muscles leading to a sinking of the chest and balancing the head freely on the spine. A tall order you might say but let's look at it in more detail.

We really start with the feet. After all they support all the rest. Are you standing on your feet or on your shoes? Where is your weight when you stand up? On your heels, your instep, the outsides of your feet, your little 'pinky' toe, your big toe ball? Where is it? You don't know because you never notice. Take your shoe off and look at the sole and heel. Where is the most worn area? How do you put your foot down? Do you 'fall' forward when you walk or do you put your foot down? You probably don't know but you can find out. This is what I meant when I was speaking about fundamental things earlier. What could be more fundamental than feet? We want to do T'ai Chi but we don't know how we stand yet.

So, stand up, tense your legs and lock your knees then slowly relax them so that they begin to bend slightly. You feel a little more comfortable. Go through this a few times so that you know the difference. Pay particular attention to your feet and how glad they feel when you unlock your knees. When you do so your feet start to relax and sink towards the ground. If you lock your knees you start to pull your feet away from the ground — a struggle against gravity which you will inevitably lose... Gravity has everything going for it and you just have your badly treated muscles.

With your knees unlocked and your feet more relaxed you can begin to spread your toes — those five stumps on the end of the feet. You can sense the shoes or the floor if you have no shoes on and find out where your weight seems to be resting. It is important to note that you are standing on your shoes. Most people, if asked where they are standing would say 'on the floor' but they are standing on their shoes, their shoes are standing on the floor and their feet on the shoes.

Now in this position you relax as much as you can. With a little pull you let your body sway a few inches forward, then with another little pull you let it sway backward and you do this a few times. Then you centre once more and pull a little to the left; a little to the right. Then centre again and sway round in a tiny circle. Right, round the circle to the front, round to the left, round and back left, round and back right and then to the front. Reverse. Then start the circle by moving backwards, left, and so on, and reverse it.

Just imagine that you are in a small boat, standing, and the water is moving very slightly, just enough to make you compensate for the changes and keep your balance. Trying this, you begin to appreciate just how little force is needed to move your body. It is quiet, it is soft, it is gentle. Just like being in a cradle again. You also notice that for once you are allowing your body some care. This is important; more important than you can guess at the beginning. This careful attention to what your body is doing is cultivated in T'ai Chi, or should be, so these apparently insignificant movements you are making in this chapter will contribute very significantly to how you perform your T'ai Chi later on.

Having tried this experiment I hope you are interested to move further. Take all your bodyweight on to the right or left foot. Let's make a decision and say right foot. Bend your knee a little, the right one, so that the right knee is over the toes of the right foot but does not protrude beyond it. Then lift your left foot, not like a pound of meat and bones but by raising your heel slowly, allowing your ankle to relax and leaving your toes on the ground. Do not lift clear yet. Just let the heel descend to the ground once more. Raise and lower the heel a few times, noticing how relaxed it can be at the ankle. That is how much force you need to raise your foot. No more.

Try the same with the right foot. By this time I hope you are even more interested in how you move. As one teacher put it, you are learning to go fifty miles to the gallon instead of five.

Return to lifting your left foot, but this time raise it clear and put it down straight in front of you. Do not bring it inwards and put it down. Put it out in the same line that it was facing. Do not stretch, or bend your trunk. Keep your weight still on your back, right, leg. Your left leg is bearing only its own weight. Now reach forward and take hold of your left kneecap. Move it from side to side and up and down. Loosen it. Straighten up and move your weight slowly on to your left leg. Do it in the same easy way as when you swayed — easy, gentle, quiet. Now your left leg is bent to take the weight and your back right leg is relaxed, 'empty'. Raise your right heel, take the leg forward, still supporting with the left leg, and loosen your right kneecap.

Then step slowly forward several times using the same loose and easy technique. Giant steps for T'ai Chi students, discovering something. Walking...

To discover more, try walking backwards in the same manner. Keep your torso vertical.

Let's move on from feet to lower leg. You will notice a thin, tough muscle and tendon running up the front and side of your shin bone. Also there are the well-known calf muscles at the back of the leg. The front one lifts the foot up towards the shin and the calf muscles push it away. They alternately contract and stretch as we walk. We don't usually notice them but now we are going to. Try the swaying exercise again and notice the action of the two muscle groups. Then try the walking and observe their action. You try to give them a holiday by letting them lose the excess tension which they have. You can tell them that it is time for a breather, a break and similar words of encouragement. By now you should be experiencing some real pleasure from this new experience in doing less. The less we do the better our T'ai Chi. We won't be able to do it well today, or tomorrow, but we are on our way.

Now turn to the knees. Earlier we unlocked the knees. Now try and see how far you can go. How far can you unlock your knees before your legs crumple. Here we come to a lot of things, and very

23

interesting they are too. Let's look at them one at a time because we are in no hurry.

As you try to unlock your knees you notice your feet. Remember we asked ourselves where our weight was placed. Sway about and find out where you feel most comfortable. If your weight moves in towards your instep you are mistaken. This action twists your knees, pulls on your inner thigh muscles, adversely affects your back — terrible. If you push outwards on to the edges of your feet, try again. Somewhere, on your feet, is your optimum position for your weight. Try to find it, noticing how your knees feel in relationship to where your weight is.

Then you look at the two lower leg groups of muscles. You watch them, in relationship to your weight on your feet and encourage them to relax too. (When I say 'watch' I mean 'be aware of'.) Then move up to your thighs and buttocks. Try shifting your weight slowly from one foot to the other. Touch your thigh muscles with the palms of your hands and notice the contraction and relaxation as your weight shifts. Same thing with your buttocks. Give all these muscles some encouraging slaps and cajole them into relaxation, and more relaxation. Begin to be a friend to your body. Don't force it. It will be a friend to you.

With perseverance you will be able to unlock your knees more and more. Now move up to the groin and pelvis/sacrum. Things are getting a bit more difficult as we move into this zone, but not impossible. A lot of research has been done into this region of the body by numbers of people interested in posture. But we can do our own.

Bend your knees a little further, keeping your palms on the small of your back and sacrum. Look at the illustration if you are unclear. I ask you to let your lower back straighten out, your abdomen to relax a little more and sink towards the fold of your groin region. Take a few deepish breaths into your lower back. This is not a breathing exercise, just a bit of encouragement to your lower back.

If you ask someone to straighten his lower back he will more than likely contract his abdomen to do it. We don't want that. We want to let the back go. So, rather than trying to do it in one movement we can encourage it by gentle bouncing up and down on our ankle and knee joints, in a playful way so that the body will not become anxious. Experiment with it and you will gradually get it. First you may contract your abdomen by mistake, or tuck your pelvis forward. What we want is to move in the direction of straightening, but with the body's agreement. If we force, then we are using muscles to pull it when what we want is a kind of acquiesence. Let's move further on up the body.

The scapula is a much neglected bone, and its muscles are not treated much better. Lift both your arms up, straight, to shoulder level. Now put your right palm on the outside of your left upper arm. The triceps muscles are there. Are they tense? Why? They are

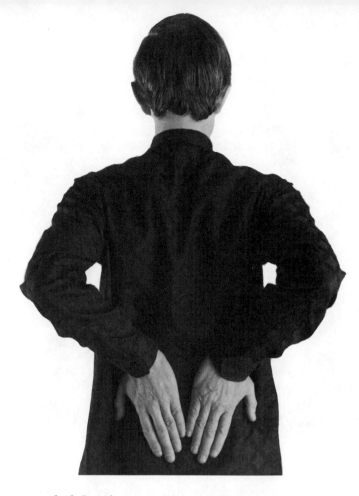

not needed. Let them go. Move on down your forearm. Is it tense? Let it go. Let your wrists go and your hand dangle.

You lift your arm with your scapula. I know that a few other muscles give it some help but the idea is to have the experience of lifting your arms from your back region, the scapula or shoulder blade region.

Go over to a chair and stand in front of it. A kitchen-type chair not an armchair. Bend your knees, keep your back in a straight line and bend from the hips, get hold of the chair and lift it, but do not bend your arms. Lift by drawing your scapulas together. Keep your arm muscles loose. Now in doing this you experience the action of your scapula. A lot of people are so tense at the shoulder that the scapula is tightly held and cannot function freely. In T'ai Chi we want to loosen the scapula. At one time I was briefly obsessed by using the scapula, but after all there are worse obsessions than that.

When the scapula is relaxed the shoulders are relaxed and the chest sinks. The back is slightly rounded. This will only come as part of an overall increased relaxation. We cannot hurry we can only try.

Some time we had to come to the head and neck. You could say, as the Alexander technique people say, that it all really depends on

 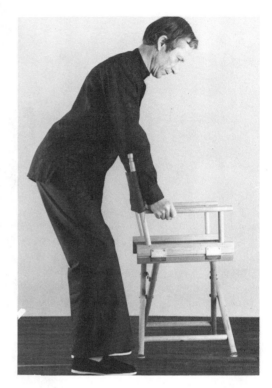

this region; that this is the key to relaxation and correct posture. Well, there is a lot of truth in that and I have deep respect for the Alexander technique. But it does not work equally well for everyone. Without doubt, though, the relationship between head and neck is very important. We can try several things. Beginning with the eyes we can keep our gaze horizontal. Do not look up or down very much when doing T'ai Chi. Then, as you let your scapulas sink you let your head 'float' up, as if, to use a traditional T'ai Chi expression, the top of your head were suspended from a thin hair. It floats up, allowing your neck to become more free.

This foregoing section will give you some hints as to approaching relaxation for T'ai Chi training. I have used a lot of words such as 'gentle', 'let', encouraging the body to respond to the new attention you are giving. This brings us, according to the Chinese, closer to the spirit of the Tao, the Way. When it feels we are interested in it the body will respond and teach us more about itself. It may even emerge, like a timid animal from its hideout, and begin to breathe more naturally. As tensions slacken, the vital process of breathing can begin to operate more freely. What a welcome experience that is. As we breathe more freely the rib cage can move, the spine is massaged as it were, the major organs of the body are touched, and we begin to feel like human beings.

Quite naturally we are being led in the direction of psychological or if you like, 'spiritual', questions. I am not spending time on those because much has been written already on these aspects. I have put a brief bibliography at the end of the book. But we can look at one word, and that is 'doing'. Everyone is busy doing, going somewhere, chasing something, retreating from something, but always doing. We are all as mad as can be. And we can't escape it just like that. But we can have a different experience of ourselves, in this case through T'ai Chi. So, when we do T'ai Chi we do not do T'ai Chi. We let the T'ai Chi do itself. When you tried the walking exercise you had an experience of what I mean. There is nothing to do; or, very, very little. So little in fact that in comparison with our daily lives it is nothing.

You were not answering the telephone, running off somewhere, going to meet your mother-in-law, no: just walking with as little effort as possible, experiencing your body and its weight and how gently you could move. To reach this it follows that your intellect and emotions are more quiet because you are paying attention to your movement. This little movement is just as important to you as the finest brush stroke of a master of Zen calligraphy. Your movement *is* your brush stroke. It leaves no visible trace but it leaves a trace on you, and you can return to it, as often as your attention will allow.

I have spent hours just moving, and so have others whom I know, and experienced the joy of not doing. T'ai Chi does itself. When you lift your arms using your scapula your arms float up, as if you were standing in a big bath and the water slowly filled the bath and raised your arms.

There is a lovely story which illustrates the spirit of what I am talking about. It is the story of the fighting cock.

Chi Hsing Tzu was raising a fighting cock for his lord. Ten days passed and the lord asked, 'Is he ready?' Chi answered, 'No, sir, he is not ready. He is still vain, and flushed with rage.' Another ten days passed, and the prince asked about the cock. Chi said, 'Not yet sir, he is alert whenever he sees the shadow of another cock or hears its crowing.' Still another ten days passed, and when the inquiry came from the prince, Chi replied, 'Not quite yet, sir. His sense of fighting is still smouldering within ready to be awakened.' When another ten days elapsed, Chi replied in response to the inquiry: 'He is almost ready. Even when he hears another crowing he shows no excitement. He now resembles one made of wood. His qualities are integrated. No cocks are his match. They will at once run away from him.' (Daisetz T. Suzuki, *Zen and Japanese Culture*, Princeton)

We are not there yet, but we are on our way.

Many famous Zen and Taoist masters used nature to illustrate either their paintings or their sayings. The natural course of water, soft and pliant yet overcoming every obstacle; the natural bend of bamboo, soft and pliant, yielding to the wind, and remaining unbroken. The awesome power of the tiger combined with smoothness of motion (and its free scapula!), its silence and majestic repose. The eternal mountains, unmoving yet alive and vibrant.

Through our lowly efforts to study T'ai Chi we can begin to tune ourselves to natural strength through relaxation and not 'doing'. Our bodies are our means of experiencing this. We study letting go, so that something different can take place.

We are not there yet, but we are on our way.

Relaxing with Partners

It is one thing to be able to relax on your own but with other people present it is something else. When another person touches you it is something else again. I devised a number of simple methods which I used with students and they seemed to have an effect in the desired direction.

1. Lie on the floor, arms and legs flat on the floor. Your partner picks up your head and raises it two or three inches. You let him or her do it. *You do not contribute to the effort yourself at all.* It is up to both of you to detect whether you contract your front neck muscles or not and interfere. Then let your partner turn your head a little from side to side, using no force, as if you were looking from left to right. Then he lowers your head to the ground. This is once more a gentle exercise.

2. You do the same type of thing with your arms and legs. Be especially careful in lifting and turning a leg not to damage the joints. It is up to the person lying down to let go of his muscles, feel the weight of the limbs concerned and generally act as if he were on a massage table allowing the masseur to loosen him up. But in this case it is mainly his own effort which is contributing to the effect, the partner is simply a kind of stimulus to provide him with a potentially richer field of experience.

3. Sit up from the floor and let your knees bend. Your partner kneels behind you and supports your back with his arms. You let go of your abdominal muscles and lean on him, as he slowly lowers your trunk to the ground. You can vary this by having your partner stand in front of you and grip your arms, and then lower you back from the front. Let go!

4. Stand up. Both arms dangle down to the sides. Your partner picks up one arm in both of his. He is allowed to move your arm and hand in any way he wishes without using undue force or going against naturally possible movement. Once again you do not 'do' anything except pay attention to letting go and allowing him to move you. Your arm is made of wood.

5.   Two people, or one person if he is strong enough, stand(s) behind you and you let yourself fall straight into the linked arms. This must be done with care as you need confidence in the people who are going to catch you, but it is well worth the minor risk involved. To wholly let oneself fall is difficult for many people but pleasant and relaxing when some experience has been gained.

6.   The above five examples will give you some idea of the direction to go in, and with a little thought and ingenuity you can devise many methods of your own. The main thing is not to do anything but allow things to be done to you. Hopefully this spirit will carry over into your T'ai Chi and foster the training in minimum effort for maximum result we are hoping for.

Experiences and Anecdotes

One amusing experience I had at the beginning of each new course of lessons was to teach people what the Alexander technique calls 'monkey' posture. In the Alexander system it is part of a course of lessons. It is also a posture of Monkey style Kung fu and so I came across it from two sources. It is not in the T'ai Chi tradition but we can use whatever helps us.

Look at the illustration and you will see that the man is standing in an ape or monkey posture with his arms and hands dangling and trunk inclined. His knees are spread giving plenty of room for his abdomen and his feet are pointing outwards. Before you go any further, let's break the 'rule' at the beginning of the book and try this. Just try that posture, maybe in front of a mirror. If you have a problem with it imagine that you have a pair of hands on your buttocks and you are reaching out for a chair you can't see. You bend your knees, incline from the hip joints and reach out for the imaginary chair. Your arms dangle, your chest is loose. Your head, back and sacrum stay in one line. That's it; get that ape feeling — like Tarzan.

If you felt strange in that posture, even a little embarrassed, you are not alone. Many students found it hard to adopt. We used to have a regular, good-natured laugh about this and speculate why. I leave you to your own speculations about this.

Try walking about in this posture, raising your legs high; swing your arms in it. Get that going through the jungle feeling and loosen up. Look at the illustration.

My strongest memory of teaching this posture was of a very well-brought up and kind young woman who could not bear this posture. She would always try to tuck her behind in. Maybe she

was right — maybe it is bad manners to stick your bottom out. But there is a time and a place for it and in our class was the time and place.

In this posture a lot of your tensions can drop away. The front of the body, the shoulders, back, legs, almost everything can have a new, free experience. Monkey posture is a useful one.

Some students felt nothing for T'ai Chi and they are not to blame for that. I found it hard to understand at first but eventually realised that it is a question of connections. Some people are connected up one way, like a telephone exchange, and some are connected up another. Some people in this 'nothing' category can relax remarkably well, but they are not aware of this fact either. They can readily attune to making minimum movement and minimum energy use but their overall reaction is 'So What?'.

Other students began to feel a positive response to relaxation but did not appreciate it enough to stay the course. It should be appreciated that T'ai Chi is a long term investment, not a quick gamble on the roulette wheel. As you slowly begin to unlock your body, over the months and years you discover new secrets about time and motion. You notice how quickly your moods can change as you move in a different way. Your concentration is sharpened and your ability to focus on doing the movements is increased. In trying circumstances this can be helpful. Some people say that you become more 'centred', more where you should be, and less dispersed into the events of life.

Let's move on to another aspect of T'ai Chi, breathing.

Breathing
The point of view I am putting here comes from an informed source, other than myself, and I recommend you to take note of it. I will enlarge on it in this chapter but it can be put briefly: avoid artificial breathing exercises.

International T'ai Chi groups and contacts have debated this question for some time but the majority favours the approach of letting the breathing follow the movement. If you attempt to 'match' your breath with your movements you can do yourself harm.

If the Tao is the natural way, then forced breathing has no place in it. If the efforts of T'ai Chi are meant to minimise effort and promote good functioning of the body then such breathing is foreign to it also. Such breathing exercises as there are, and there are many both in books and different kinds of health (?) classes, may have a place in systems of human development where a student is constantly under the guidance of a teacher who understands what he is doing. But to put them in a book and leave people to get on with them is nothing short of a crime — at best a display of chronic ignorance and lack of conscience.

For an excellent presentation of a different attitude from what is common today towards the subject of breathing exercises you should read the chapter 'Ekim Bey' in the book *Meetings with Remarkable Men* by G. I. Gurdjieff, Routledge & Kegan Paul. Here is an extract:

> By artificially changing our breathing, we change first of all the tempo of the functioning of our lungs, and, as the activity of the lungs is connected, among other things, with the activity of the stomach, the tempo of functioning of the stomach is also changed, at first slightly and then more and more. For the digestion of food, the stomach needs a certain time: let us say that food must remain there an hour. But if the tempo of the stomach's function is changed, then the time for the passing of the food through the stomach is also changed: the food may pass through so quickly that the stomach has only time to do a part of what it has to do. It is the same with the other organs. That is why it is a thousand times better to do nothing with our organism. Better leave it damaged than try to repair it without knowing how.

That is what we do in T'ai Chi: nothing:

The classical view of breathing in T'ai Chi is that when the body is more relaxed the breath will follow of its own accord, as a calf will follow a mother cow, to obtain what is naturally its own. You do not have to coerce the calf and you do not have to coerce your breath. Longer and more relaxed breaths have been noted in deep states of meditation when the mind is more still and is known in T'ai Chi as the 'breath of the turtle'. It fills the trunk and harmonises with the movements.

Here is another example of views on breathing, this time from T'ai Chi instructor Douglas Lee: 'Do not force breathing to fit into form and movement... The human body is so synchronised that the need for oxygen in the body cells and rate of delivery by the respiratory and cardiovascular system to these cells is automatically regulated.'

He goes on to list resulting upsets of forced breathing, including shortages of oxygen in the blood and acid/base unbalance in the body's biochemistry. When you relax your scapulas and your shoulders sink down you are permitting your body to breathe more easily. When you allow your abdomen more freedom you give your diaphragm more opportunity. By creating the right conditions within your body through relaxation then the body's own mechanisms can operate more healthily. Edward Maisel, in his book, *T'ai Chi for Health*, quotes a certain Elizabeth Beit, who worked for ten years in several prestigious hospitals in the USA as a respiratory technician. She said, 'Breathing is not something to be superimposed on experience. It should arise, as in T'ai Chi, in answer to the infinitely precise exigencies of experience.' I hope that you are beginning to get the message about breath, as relevant quotations pile up. They are all useful as they present the views of different, independent people who have come to the same conclusions, often through different routes.

A point you may have noticed yourself is that if you try to breathe in a different way it makes more work for the heart. When we are relaxed, the heartbeat naturally slows down, the amount of adrenalin in the bloodstream diminishes and we move closer to the repairing the body state that we reach in a good sleep. When we force our breath we are putting the body in an alarming situation. It does not know why it is being either force fed or starved since the change in the breathing has been put on it by the mind, who read it in a book or heard it from someone or other. The mind is constantly dreaming things up for the body to do, without consulting it at all. This time, we are using our mind to tell our mind not to interfere with the body breath.

The most famous T'ai Chi teacher in the West was Chen Man-ch'ing. He wrote: 'Ultimately, the breathing becomes such an intrinsic part of the exercise that you will not even have to think of it.'

His even more famous teacher — in China and Hong Kong that is — Master Yang Ch'eng-fu, used to tell him at least ten times a day: 'Relax, relax, be calm. Release the whole body.'

Let's look at this question of breath from a completely different angle. We are surrounded by air. It exerts a certain pressure at a certain altitude. It is much smaller than the water pressure when we dive into a deep pool or swim under water but it exists just the same. When we exhale there is a partial vacuum in the lungs. It is partial because we never completely empty our lungs when breathing. To fill this vacuum we do not have to draw in the air. The existing partial vacuum is filled by the existing air pressure. It is done for us. In T'ai Chi we do nothing. When anyone walks up a steep hill he needs more oxygen for the extra work he is doing. Then the automatic adjustment is made by the body and it does draw in air. The pressure of the air and the slower, more quiet experience of T'ai Chi breathing are not adequate for such exertions. But on the other hand, when exertion is reduced to a minimum a different mechanism operates.

Since I began to write this book I have referred to many sources and some of them appear to contradict what I have been saying about breath. For instance, Liu Hui-ching wrote: '...a beginner is taught to inhale while the hand-arm movements are moving upward, forward and outward, and to exhale while they are moving downward, backward and inward.'

I find this unbelievable, which is why I said 'appear to contradict'. For one thing a beginner has all his work cut out to perform the movements correctly. It is impossible that he should be asked to match his breath and arms. There are statements with similar defects in them, in other sources. I call them defects because I think they are possibly errors of expression rather than meaning. I would hope that Liu, quoted above, meant to say that a beginner, when he has learned the movements, accurately enough, and is more relaxed, sees that his breath tends to follow the pattern quoted. It does naturally happen, doesn't it, that if you raise your arms above your head you tend to breathe in, and when you bend or draw your arms towards your body you tend to breathe out? I prefer to interpret what Liu said in this way and I advise you to do the same.

Another note on breath and then we leave it for a while. If you read books on Zen, for instance *Zen Training*, by Katsuki Sekida, you will inevitably come across references to breathing, such as counting the breath, tidal air and abdominal tension. You may well ask me, a mere Englishman, and not a Zen master, if I am daring to say that all the Zen masters are wrong and I am right. That they are wrong to teach breath changes. They are not wrong. All we need is some thought about the situation, and about the people involved, because there is no such thing as breath on its own, only breathing people. Many of us do not think very much, we are more like parrots than people; here is what I mean.

Take three people. One is an absolute newcomer to Zen, to T'ai Chi or anything similar. Two is a T'ai Chi student with a good teacher. Three is a Zen student with an experienced Zen master looking out for him. It is plain to see that each of these three students is in a different situation. To offer each of them a book with Zen breathing exercises could produce three entirely different results. The first may read such a book and try to change his breath on his own. It is probably accurate to say he would produce adverse effects. The second, under his teacher's eye, could make sure he is not forcing his breathing and may find the results anticipated. The third has already been trained along similar lines to what is presented in the book, and in any case he has his teacher. He is following an *experience* similar to his own. His master knows what he is experiencing and can guide him. When Katsuki Sekida writes about the different flows of breath he is writing about what he *experienced*. But for an outsider to read and then try to impose another's experience on his own is a different matter. It seems to me like trying to make your foot fit the shoe instead of a shoe which fits the foot.

I hope I have convinced you about avoiding artificial breathing exercises.

Experiences and Anecdotes
When I first began to learn to do T'ai Chi my teacher taught me to breathe in a certain way; in, when raising the arms and out, when lowering them. He also taught me to move at a certain tempo allotting so many 'beats' to each position and connecting movement. Looking back I see that this was a mistake. At times I

experienced pressure in my chest and even dizziness. I stopped all this and just went back to moving and relaxing. I still have the notes I made at the time and can say that what might have been a good tempo for him, a man of taller build and heavier bone structure, was not suitable for me. I think he was very keen for me to make progress and this influenced his judgement; or maybe he meant me to keep his advice for later and I jumped the gun.

I just mention this because if you turn to a teacher to learn T'ai Chi you should always use your own commonsense combined with what he tells you. As I said at the beginning we should not regard all teachings from the East as coming from all-wise and benevolent men who understand everything about all things. We do both them and ourselves an injustice by this uncritical attitude.

Another story is about a very lovely girl who came to my classes. She was in love with one of the men in the class. She learned to do the movements better than anyone else. It was a sheer delight to watch her. Her breathing and postures just co-ordinated very naturally and I was amazed at her progress. I believe her feeling for the man helped her to travel so fast in her study. Then her relationship with the man fell apart. Her T'ai Chi turned to dust and soon after she left the class. The man continued to come and learn more. He was greedy for more. He wanted to learn more and more movements. Each week he would ask me, 'What comes next?' I would tell him to be patient and try to perfect what he already knew. He learned the Long Form in about one year and went off to start his own class. But, when I last saw him he still had not relaxed enough to move as well as his former girl friend.

This urgent requirement to learn more and more is to be expected. But it shows a failure to understand that T'ai Chi is more concerned with deepening our experience of ourselves and less with doing more and more.

One teacher told me that in Taiwan there was a monk who did just two movements which were for him the equivalent of the performance of the whole Long Form. I relate this with the idea of deepening experience rather than simply extending it. Perhaps this monk's perception of himself was so profound that he could experience in two simple movements what it took another person 108 movements to experience.

Let's move on to the movements of T'ai Chi themselves. I hope you will resist the temptation to start doing them right away and read and understand the book all the way through first. Here we go...

FORM AND MEANING

All traditional martial arts and exercises have at their core what is generally referred to as a Form. In Japanese it is called *Kata*, in Korean *Hyung*, and is sometimes also translated into English as pattern or set. One of the purposes of a Form is that it can serve as a reservoir or dictionary because the Forms of any particular system contain all the techniques of that system. A student can go to the Form for a technique if he wishes. Another purpose of the Form is to familiarise the student, imprint on the student the techniques and show him methods of combining them in different ways.

Schools of Karate have many Forms, as do schools of swordsmanship, but in T'ai Chi there is usually only one central Form which is learned and trained in over and over. When doing a Form, certain 'finished' postures are reached, but they are reached or strung together in different ways. This has led some people to call Form a dance, but this is a mistake and conveys the wrong spirit to whoever hears it for the first time. The only way in which a Form can be said to resemble a dance is that they both consist of continuous movement.

A third purpose of a Form is to gradually imbue the student with the spirit of the school, the foundation of the school. For instance, some schools of Karate are very powerful, using a great deal of swift, tough, muscular movements. Others are light, speedy and graceful. The same applies to Kung fu and to a lesser extent to T'ai Chi. Some styles of T'ai Chi have a combat orientation whilst others are almost entirely therapeutic. The Form we are studying here is for both. But in this book we are concentrating on relaxation, softness and naturalness.

It is said that when T'ai Chi first began there was no continuous Form. Different postures, static positions were taught, and ways of assuming and leaving them. Then, it is said, teachers decided to join them together and produce an unbroken, flowing sequence. Since it is the hardest part of learning T'ai Chi Form to connect the postures together, I suggest that when you come to try to train you take each posture from a neutral standing position and then another until you know all of them. Only then begin to connect them according to instructions.

Preliminary Movements
Before we touch the Form let's have a look at moving again. I want you to imagine that your feet are the two triangles standing on the rectangle shown. Your feet are pointing north and you are looking north. Stand up and stand on this imaginary rectangle. Simple. Now step with your left foot on to the north-west corner, placing your foot down *before* you shift your weight on to it. The rectangle is about the same width as your shoulders so your feet remain

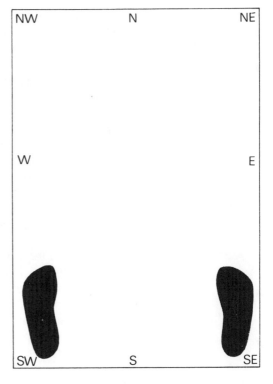

shoulder width apart (remember the railway lines). There is no strain and you only use as much force as is needed. Now turn your right foot out, 45 degrees to the right. Your left foot is pointing north on the north-west corner and your right foot is pointing north-east on the south-east corner. Your front left knee is bent and your rear right knee is almost straight.

This sounds and looks over-complicated at first but it is not. It is a question of getting it right from the beginning. You may not need all the compass points, but someone else might. It is worth noting that some teachers actually require their students to face a particular direction as they believe that some kind of force comes from that direction and helps in training. Now move your left foot back to its former position at south-west and turn your right foot back in so that it is pointing north from the south-east corner. Repeat this sequence putting your right foot forward.

This finished leg position is very common to T'ai Chi Form and needs to be learned so that it is second nature.

Check: Feet shoulder width apart to begin — front foot pointing forward — rear foot 45 degrees out turn — most weight on front foot — rear leg slightly bent and front leg bent to take weight. Your front knee never goes beyond the toe of your front foot as beyond this point you are almost off balance and cannot draw your weight back.

Have you got it?

Stand in the position shown in the photograph. This is the same one we just did. Now slowly shift your weight on to your rear leg, and slide your front foot back a few inches, raising the heel a little but toes on the ground. Your rear leg is slightly bent to take the weight. We call this the Toe stance.

Check: weight mostly on rear foot — rear foot turned out 45 degrees leg bent — front foot heel raised — front leg bends naturally.

Just as driving a car in Britain for an American consists merely in keeping to the left hand side of the road, so performing T'ai Chi consists of remembering these two stances, especially the first. We shall make a few turns, reverse, park, and so on, but if the feet of the Form are right we are almost home. You will be unique if you can remember that without a lot of reminders.

Now let's have a look at turning. This too is crucial when you come to connect one of the postures with another. Turning and stepping in T'ai Chi are different from turning and stepping across a room or down a street. Whenever we turn and step in T'ai Chi we *shift weight*.

Stand in the first completed posture again, that is, the first stance. Your weight is evenly divided between the feet. This is just a preliminary position because in T'ai Chi we never have the feet evenly weighted. This is called 'double weighting' and is to be avoided. It is a vulnerable position from the point of view of keeping balance if pushed; more on this later.

To correct this we gently shift weight on to the left leg, using as much force as for pushing aside a blade of grass. Your right foot is in contact with the floor but bears almost no weight. Now push your weight back on to your right foot. Do this a few times to gain the experience. This is like the walking forward we did earlier. The foot is put in place *and then* we shift weight. It is not like ordinary walking.

Now the turn, go back to the position shown in the diagram — the first step you took. With the weight on the left leg, turn your right foot and waist a further 45 degrees to the right so that it is pointing east. Both feet are temporarily at right angles to one another. Left to north and right to east. It is simple. Now gradually shift your weight on to the right foot, turning your waist and trunk completely to the right so that you are facing east, and turn your rear left foot in 45 degrees.

This is a moment for a piece of observation and thought which does not strike everyone immediately. You will note now that you are standing in the same position as when you started but your opposite leg is leading and you have turned 90 degrees right or east. It happens all the time. In T'ai Chi we are always doing it; shifting weight and turning from one direction to another, almost always in the same fashion. Now without any assistance find your way back to the previous stance, in the correct way.

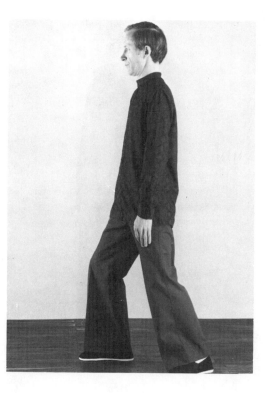 

Did you find your way back? Yes? No?

Let's check.

You kept your weight on your leading right foot.

You turned your left foot back 90 degrees

This meant it was pointing north again.

You shifted your weight gently back on to your left leg.

You turned your right foot in 45 degrees.

You found yourself back in the correct position.

Do these changes a few times to the right and then try doing them to the left, beginning with the right foot in the north-east corner pointing north and the left foot in the south-west corner pointing out 45 degrees north-west. If you can do these turns fluently then you are ready to move into the Form which we shall tackle without more ado. Get the feet right and the hands will take care of themselves.

1. Preparation Posture

In this posture we break the rule about double weighting. Weight is evenly distributed on both feet — but never again. Your feet are parallel to one another about three inches apart. I suggest your shoulders should be loosened, your knees slackened, your head turned a few times, and so on to 'break' any tensions you produce at the beginning. These looseners are not part of the Preparation posture but not many people can take a position and relax immediately. Once this has been done you stand quietly in place.

With training you will be able to stand still without any preliminaries and relax quietly with no visible movements.

Now shift your weight on to your right foot in the manner described earlier in the book and raise your left foot, heel first. Place it away to the left so that both feet are shoulder width apart. As you do this you take both your arms out away from your body at the elbows by bending them slightly. Imagine you are holding a large egg under each armpit. Then shift 50 per cent of your weight on to your left foot, so that both feet are parallel, facing forward, shoulder width apart, knees slightly bent, back straight, and look horizontally forward.

Once again, since you are just learning the Form first and not performing it, I suggest you loosen up as described above, once again, because the concentration of following this entirely new way of moving produces tension and it needs eliminating at each step of the way. Once you have the Form committed to memory

41

you can concentrate on reducing tension as you move. I will not keep repeating this. Just do it after or even before each posture from now on, until you no longer feel that it helps you.

2. Beginning

Here comes the scapula. Using your scapulas, raise your arms out in front of you. Or alternatively we can say you should let them float up as suggested earlier. Your wrists dangle on the ends of your arms. When the arms have reached a horizontal position you withdraw them slowly, straightening your wrists and then lowering your elbows back to your sides. Your palms descend past your elbows and return to their original position.

Just stop here, and perform the arms raising with one arm. Use the other to feel your scapula. Before you move your raised arm your scapula edge may stick out a bit from your back. But as you raise your arm, from your back, your scapula should slide forward over your rib cage and 'flatten' against it. Your arm muscles should be almost flaccid or very relaxed. A fault which creeps in at this point, and in all cases where the arms are raised and lowered is leaving the scapula and shoulder 'raised' even when the arms are lowered. Pay as much attention to lowering your arms correctly as you do to raising them.

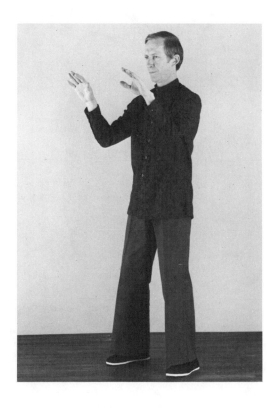

3. Holding the Ball

Shift most of your weight on to your left foot in the recommended fashion, using minimum effort. As you do so turn your waist to the east (right), simultaneously turning your right foot so that the toe is raised an inch or so from the ground. Your left hand travels up in a curve, palm up, across the front of your left groin and right lower abdomen, coming to a rest cupped above your right hip bone. As your left hand moves your right hand rises above it, elbow lowered, so that you finish up as if holding a big ball. Move your arms via your scapula.

4. Ward off Left

Now shift your weight on to your right foot, so that it is flat on the ground. When most of it is on your right foot you raise the heel of your left foot and turn your waist slowly back towards the north (left), stepping forward with your left foot on to the north-west (top left) corner of the rectangle we have met earlier. Remember to place the heel of the foot down first and then flat. Only then do you shift your weight on to it. As you shift your weight, raise your left arm across your body and lower your right arm, finally turning your right foot in 45 degrees. See the photograph for the posture.

When you read instructions like these it seems complicated. It

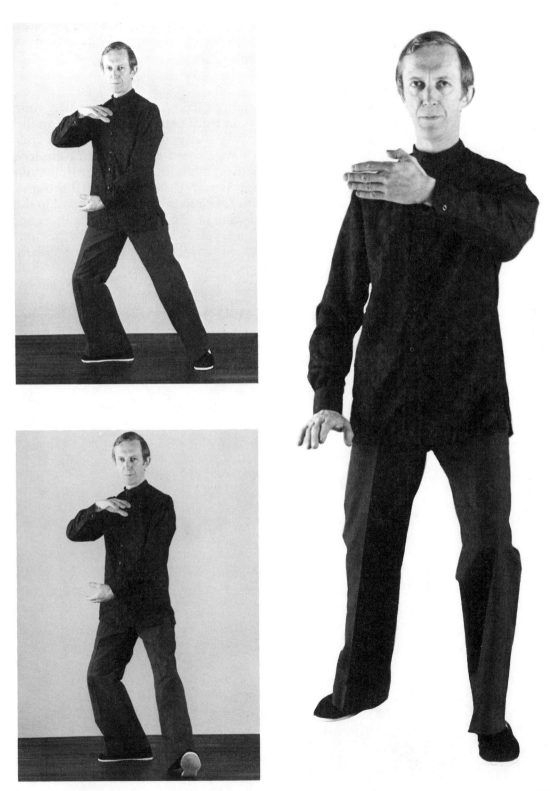

isn't really. All you have been doing with your feet is the simple stepping exercise you did earlier with the feet alone. The arms follow the changes in the foot positions.

5. Ward off Right

Now shift almost all your weight on to your left foot, turning your left palm to face down, and your right palm up, as in holding the ball but with opposite hands. Whilst you do this you turn your waist to the east (right) and step forward an inch, your right foot pointing directly east. This movement is little more than adjusting the foot as it remains more or less in the same place. Shift your weight forward on to the right foot, raising your right hand to the position shown, and the left palm facing it. The left arm does not really move forward. As you shift your weight and turn to the right it moves in with the body. It *seems* to move but it does not. Finally turn in your left foot 45 degrees.

6. Roll-back

Turn your waist a little towards the south-east (right) keeping your foot position stable and weight distribution unchanged. Turn the left palm up again and bring it to a position about four inches from your right elbow. The right hand stays high and the palm turns into an inclined downward facing position. Then you

'roll-back' slowly on to your left foot and turn your waist to the left — feet unmoved. When this waist turn has brought your navel facing north (front) you release your left arm. It goes down from the elbow and back up once more, resting lightly on your right palm, so that the heels of both hands fit snugly together. As you make the arm movement you slowly turn back to face east (right) once more, but your weight still remains on your left leg. Once established in this position you are ready to make the next simple move.

7. Press

Slowly shift your weight forward on to your right leg, and as your weight is taken by that leg you extend your arms a little, from the scapula, then extend your arms a little from the elbow, as if pressing against a surface with the back of your right hand.

8. Withdraw and Push

Your right hand turns down and out so that the palm is facing east (away from you), then separate your hands, shifting your weight once more on to your rear leg. Your palms retract nearer your chest, facing away from you. When you are 'settled' on to your rear leg you push out again, shifting your weight, extending from scapula and then elbow, as if pushing on a surface with both palms. Some people say that the push in the palms should not be equal, so that you are not double weighting with the palms.

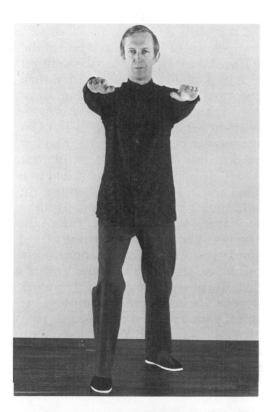

9. Single Whip

This is the most distinguishing posture of T'ai Chi and one of the most difficult to describe. But if we take it step by step we shall get it. Shift your weight once more back on to your left foot and turn your right foot in, turning your waist at the same time. Your arms, by straightening your elbows and palms, are held almost horizontally away from you. As arms are never fully extended in T'ai Chi then they bend a little. In this arms out posture you turn as far left as you can, from the waist, as one unit. Then begin to shift your weight back on to your right foot. Bring your left hand down in a curve, to end palm up near your waist. As you do this your right hand forms a 'beak', fingers and thumb together, and bends at the wrist. Your hand relationship is as in Holding the Ball. Your right hand comes in closer to your body as you gently turn on the toes of your left foot, and then the hand goes out towards the north-east. Supporting yourself on your right leg, step out and round towards the west with your left leg. Place the heel on the ground. The toe is pointing west. As you shift your weight on to the left leg, the whole foot touching the ground, your left palm rises across your body, past your eyes, and out to follow the foot. You watch it with your eyes, intently. The palm finally turns to face west. Your right foot should already be turned in 45 degrees. You are now in Single Whip posture.

54

When you try to do the Form, I advise you to aim to reach Single Whip and train until you are familiar with the Form up to that point. Otherwise, if you try to drag your way further through you will forget what you have to do and become confused.

10. Lifting Hands

Now we have a simple posture again. Shifting your weight completely on to your left leg, and turning your waist to face north again, bring your right foot in so that is in line with your left heel. Your right foot rests on its heel, toes slightly raised. As you do this bring your arms in and down, by using the scapulas again, both being bent at the elbow. Imagine you are playing a guitar but left handedly.

11. Shoulder Stroke or Lean Forward

Though sometimes called Lean Forward you do not actually lean in this posture as in T'ai Chi the trunk is upright. Bring your right foot back to rest on the ball of the toes and lower your hands in front of your groin. As you step out once more with the right foot, in the same direction, place your left hand, palm down, near the inside fold of your right elbow. Shift your weight on to your right foot, keeping arms stable. Remember to put the heel of the right foot down first.

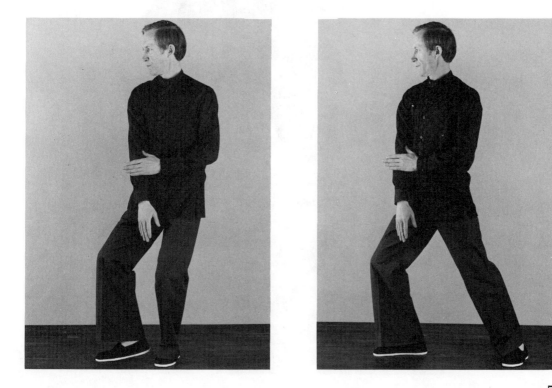

12. White Crane Spreads Wings

With most of your weight on your right foot from the Shoulder Stroke posture your left leg turns on the ball of the foot, to the west (left). As it does so, you lower your left palm to a position above but slightly outside your left knee-thigh region. Palm is down but not hanging; the hand is bent back slightly at the wrist. As the left arm descends the right rises on the inside of it, making a curve up from the left lower side of the body to outside the right temple, and above it. The palm faces outwards.

56

13. Brush Left Knee and Twist Step

Lower your left heel but still keep your weight on your right foot. At the same time circle your left palm clockwise (as if you were looking at the clock), raising it about twelve inches above your left knee. It brushes or almost brushes your left knee — 'almost' because a person's arms do not reach his knees in a vertical posture. As you begin this left hand movement you take a little step west with the left foot. At the same time rotate your right arm inwards from the elbow/shoulder/scapula and lower it towards your right knee, take it back and bring it up and past your right ear, palm down. As you complete your brushing and stepping with the left limbs and your hand comes past your right ear, shift your weight on to your left leg.

When you see someone doing T'ai Chi correctly, it looks as though he is moving his arms a lot. He is not. He is moving his body a lot and his arms very little. As you shift weight on to your left leg the right palm comes forward, mainly because your body weight is moving. Finally extend a little from scapula and elbow.

14. Play Guitar

Shift most of your weight back on to your left foot and raise your right foot, taking a slight step to the right with your foot turned in 30 degrees. Then shift most of your weight on to it and bring your left foot, heel only touching, so that it is in line with the heel of your right, and seems straight, though it is slightly bent. Your palms come in to the similar position shown in Lifting Hands — this time playing a guitar right handedly.

15. Brush Left Knee and Twist Step

Repeat the movement for 13 except the left hand just circles down in front of the left knee.

16. Step forward, Deflect downward, Intercept and Punch

These are four movements ending in a 'punch' posture, but without the force of a blow. The arm and hand merely assume a punching position.

Shift your weight back on to your right foot, and lower your right hand, lightly clenched, across and over your left thigh, turning your left foot out 45 degrees. Take your left hand back in a circle and shift your weight on to your left foot. At the same time raise your right fist, palm down, in a semi-circle in front of your waist.

As left and right hands reach the top of their respective circles step out to the right with your right foot and take the right fist downward palm up as if parrying a punch — but softly of course. The left hand continues its own arc and also deflects an imaginary blow coming along the same trajectory as that which the right deflected or parried.

To complete this series step forward in a straight line with the left foot and shift your weight on to it. At the same time, turn your waist into a forward facing position and turn your right foot in 45 degrees. Your hands accompany your feet, not moving independently. As you turn forward facing, your right fist passes over your right hip and out in the same direction as your left foot. Your left hand, palm in, 'swings' out with the same waist turn.

61

17. Withdraw and Push

Shift your weight on to your right leg and open your right fist. Draw back both arms so that they form an X-shape facing your chest with your palms. Shift your weight back on to your left leg, turning both palms out and away from you. At the end of the shift weight movement extend arms with scapula and elbow.

Take care, I remind you, not to send your left knee beyond your left toes.

18. Cross Hands

Shift most of your weight back on to your right foot and turn your waist north (right). As you turn, your right palm, facing away from you, makes an arc about six inches above your right forehead, to the right. Your left palm, in conjunction with your right, facing away from you, makes a lower arc, to the left. When your weight is mostly on your right foot, and as you turn your waist north, the left foot turns inwards on the heel, so that it lines up north also. Then shift most weight over on to the left foot. Your arms have continued to make their downward arcs until they can go no further, then they come inwards, cross and rise in front of the chest, palms in, right on the outside. Draw your right foot back, shoulder width from your left, parallel with the left. Two-thirds weight is on the left foot, one-third on the right.

Note: Though words occur one after the other on the printed page, these movements must all be synchronised, flowing together. If you remember that the feet and body are the leaders of the movement and the hands and arms are secondary you will soon get the 'right' feel of T'ai Chi movement.

In the Long Form this is the first quarter of the sequence and I advise you to train up to the Crossing Hands position until you have the sequence by heart. Go over the earlier points about relaxation, minimum effort, foot position, stepping, and so on, to make sure that in your pursuit of learning the Form you have not forgotten the fundamentals. Keep your knees loose.

19. Embrace Tiger and Return to Mountain

Lower your weight a little by bending your knees. Lower both hands, turning the right palm to face down but left palm still facing up. As your hands descend, begin to turn your waist to the right. Shift weight on to the left foot, completely, and step right round with your right foot to the south-east (back right corner). This will necessitate good balance on the left leg, 'opening' the whole area between your hips to give freedom of movement, and 'reaching' round with the right foot. As you step round with the right foot, bring the left palm in a circle past your left ear, and brush above the right knee as it is planted, with the right palm. You continue

with this movement by shifting your weight on to your right foot, turning your right palm to face upwards above your right thigh, and slightly outside it. Push forward with your left palm in front of your eyes.

20. Still facing the south-east, repeat the Roll-back movement which you now know (6).

21. Continue with Press movement which you now know (7).

22. Continue with Withdraw and Push (8).

23. Continue with Single Whip which will bring you facing north-west.

24. Punch Under Elbow
This is a very agreeable and 'wide open' movement. Shift your weight on to your right leg and open your beak hand from Single Whip posture. Lower both your palms so that the arms are horizontal, facing down. Then with your weight on your right foot you take your left over to the west (left) pointing position. Begin by shifting your weight on to that leg and at the same time turn your waist so that your arms move in conjunction with it. As you reach

your most forward weight shifting position you turn in your right foot to the 45 degree position. At this point your left arm will be pointing roughly out to your left side, south, and your right arm to the west (in front of you).

Lift your right foot and replace it, as if adjusting your foothold, and take your left palm behind you as if scooping up a handful of rice. Bring it up, in front of you, and at the same time 'brush' your right palm down the outer edge of your ascending left arm. As your 'brushing' right palm reaches the elbow of the left arm it forms a light fist, and remains as if supporting the left arm. Whilst the arms are moving to their completed position you place your weight back on to your right foot and the left foot rests on its heel in front of you, leg almost straight. You are facing west.

25. Step back to Drive the Monkey away
Open your right fist, take it back in a curve past your right thigh and up near your right ear, palm down. At the same time extend your left arm downwards, palm up, elbow slightly bent. Remember to use your scapulas as you move, keep your shoulders down and move with minimum effort. As you complete this movement step back with your left foot. Shift your weight slowly backwards on to your left foot, and push out with the right palm in front of your eyes. Your left palm comes back close to your left thigh, palm still

up. As you complete the posture turn your right foot into a straight line pointing west.

26.   Step back to Drive Monkey away — opposite side
Circle your left palm back and up to your left ear, palm down. Bring your right palm down, palm up, close to your right thigh and step back with your right foot, completing a similar posture to 25. but with opposite hands and feet.

27.   Step back to Drive the Monkey away — opposite side
Repeat the movements and posture of 25.

28. Diagonal Flying Posture

Take your right palm down near your left hip bone and bring your left palm back and up on top of the right as if holding a ball again. Sit down a little more on your left leg and open your abdomen and groin area to take a large step right round to the north-east (right); begin to shift your weight on to it. At the same time bring your right palm up and across in front of your body, and away from you, so that it is raised, palm up, in front of your eyes. Keep it slightly bent; use your scapula. As you raise your right arm, your left sweeps gently down and back with palm turned towards the back. Turn in your left foot.

 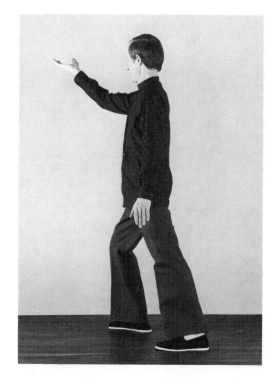

29. Waving Hands in the Clouds

Bring your right palm down in front of your right armpit and your left palm below it, holding an imaginary ball once more. At the same time take a short step north with your left foot so that it is pointing directly north. Your weight is still on your right foot.

Turn your waist and dip your right palm out and down in a curve to near your right hip and bring your left palm up near your right shoulder. As your waist turns, both palms pass in front of your body, right below left. When they reach the left side you shift your weight on to your left foot and turn the right foot in so that it is parallel with the left.

30. Waving Hands in the Clouds – opposite side
You begin this movement with the same Holding the Ball position as in 29. except that your left hand is on top at the beginning but immediately dips down to your left hip and the right circles above it, holding the ball again. Turn your waist to the right and when your hands have moved across to the right side shift your weight on to the right foot and take a small step sideways with the left foot, keeping it parallel to the right.

31. Waving Hands in the Clouds
Repeat the movements of 29. without the initial adjusting steps.

32. Single Whip
To move from 31. into the Single Whip take a short step north-east with the right foot and shift weight on to it. At the same time raise the right hand into a beak and continue with the movements of 9.

33.   Single Whip Squatting down

Your right foot turns out and you shift your weight back on to it.
Keep the beak hand in the same position and sit down on to your
right leg as far as you comfortably can. As you do so turn your left
foot in and bring your left palm back, in a vertical plane, to your
left inner thigh. Shift your weight forward again and slide your left
palm along above your left leg as far as you comfortably can.

This is not a beginner's posture, in fact, and I know few Western
people, including myself, who can do it as well as Chinese who
have learned from the cradle. Do not try at first to sit down far as
you can injure both right knee and lower back. Your whole body
needs to 'get to know' this posture.

34.   Golden Cockerel Stands on One Leg

Continue to push forward from the last posture and shift your
weight on to the left leg, turning it slightly outwards. Your left
palm goes up vertically and then descends to your left thigh whilst
your right leg rises up, knee bent and foot relaxed down. Your
right beak hand is opened into an open palm and comes up with
your leg into a vertical position, elbow above the knee.

35. Golden Cockerel Stands on One Leg — opposite side
Step gently down with your right foot, behind you, foot pointing slightly out and raise your left knee as in 34. but opposite side. Lower your right palm, downward facing, and raise your left palm inside it, inward facing, bending at the elbow, poised above the left knee.

36. Separate Right Foot

Place your left foot gently down behind you and slowly move your weight on to it. Lower your left palm, upwards facing, and turn your waist south, bringing your right palm down and up, under your left, so that the forearms make an X-shape. Your waist turns round to the right to face the north-west and the X-shaped arms rise up in front of your chest and face. You 'kick' gently up with your right foot to just above knee height, taking your open right hand forward in line with your leg and your left open hand back diagonally.

37.   Separate Left Foot
Lower your right foot near your left, still pointing north-west. Shift your weight forward on to your right foot. Bring both arms down and round in circle, facing in, as in 36. but with left palm outside the right. Turn your trunk to face south-west and as you separate your palms as in 36. you kick out with your left foot.

38.   Turn and Strike with Heel
Do not put your left foot back down on the ground after 37. Just lower your leg from the knee so that it points straight down. Your left thigh is parallel with the floor. Bring your arms circling down once more as in 36. As they come back to your body you swivel on your right heel to your left so that you face east. Kick out east with your left foot, using the heel. This is more like a push away from you with your foot rather than your notion of a kick as such. As you kick, use the arms as in Separate Left Foot, 37.

39.   Step down and Brush Left Knee and Twist Step
Step down with your left foot placing the heel first and repeat the movements of 13.

40.   Brush Right Knee and Twist Step

Shift your weight on to your right foot, turning your left toes out as you do so. As you turn out, your right palm, down facing, comes across to your left waist, and your left palm moves out away to your left side. Shift your weight forward on to your left foot and step forward with your right foot, pointing directly forward. As you now shift your weight on to your right foot you 'brush' your right knee with your right palm and bring your left palm past your left ear and out in front of your eyes. This movement is simply the opposite of 39.

41.   Step forward and Punch with Fist

Shift your weight back on to your left foot and bring your left palm, down facing, across your chest. At the same time turn out your right foot and make a light fist with your right hand, drawing it back to your right hip. Shift your weight on to your right leg and step forward with your left leg, pointing directly forward. As you now shift your weight on to your left leg you lightly brush your left thigh with your left palm and punch diagonally downward with your right fist, inclining the whole trunk slightly forward. This is an exceptional deviation from the vertical posture maintained throughout the Form.

42. Step forward and Ward off Right

Shift your weight on to your right foot and turn your left foot out. Shift your weight on to your left foot and step forward directly on to your right foot, forward facing. As you do so, keep your weight back on your turned out left foot. Take both arms away to your left in a curve and repeat the final arm movements and leg movements of 5., including the weight shift — right foot.

43. Roll-Back — repeat movement 6.

44. Press — repeat movement 7.

45. Withdraw and Push — repeat movement 8.

46. Single Whip — repeat movement 9.

47. Fair Lady Works with Shuttles

Shift most of your weight on to your right foot and turn your left foot in on the heel as far as you can, so that you are more or less 'pincer-toed'. The turning in of your left foot is accompanied by a turning of the whole trunk from the waist and an opening of the beak of the right hand. When you reach the limit of your turn, your right foot opens out as you shift your weight on to your left leg. Your right palm rotates into an upward facing position whilst your left palm comes across your body to lie just below your right armpit, palm up.

Shift your weight on to your right foot and step forward with your left foot, diagonally. As you now shift your weight on to your left foot you withdraw your right leading arm and slide your left palm forward a few inches below it in the same direction as your leading foot. Completing both your weight shift and the arm movements, turn both palms to face away from you.

You are now in a position with both arms raised, your left higher than your right, as if protecting your face. To complete this movement you gently turn your waist a little to the left and push out with your right palm and draw back your left a little.

48. Fair Lady Works with Shuttles — opposite side

Shift your weight on to your right leg. Turn in with your left foot to the pincer-toe position. As you do so your raised left palm comes across and above your forehead and your right palm goes down close to and below your left elbow, upward facing. Shift your weight back on to the left foot, releasing the right, and turn out with the right foot. Step out a short step diagonally with your right foot, and as you shift your weight on to it withdraw your left arm and slide your right along and under it, a few inches below, palm up. When the right palm reaches the end of your left arm it rises, palm away from you and pulls back a little, above your right temple. At the same time as it draws back the left pushes forward beyond it, and once more the hands are held in a kind of protective position.

49.   Fair Lady Works with Shuttles — opposite side
Shift weight back on to the left leg and turn in the right foot, then step out diagonally with the left, repeating the movements of 47.

50.   Fair Lady Works with Shuttles — opposite side
Repeat 48.

51.   Ward off Left
Bring both hands down into the Holding the Ball position with the right hand on top, at the right side of the body. Turn the waist to the north and step round with the left foot to point north. Raise the left arm up across the body, palm in and lower the right close to the thigh. Turn in the right foot 45 degrees.

52.   Ward off Right — repeat movement 5.

53.   Roll-Back — repeat movement 6.

54.   Press — repeat movement 7.

55.   Withdraw and Push — repeat movement 8.

56.   Single Whip — repeat movement 9.

57.   Single Whip Squatting down — repeat movement 33.

58.   Step forward to the Seven Stars
Shifting most of your weight on to your left foot you rise and take a short step forward with your right foot. Your beak hand opens and moves forward along with your right foot. It forms a light fist and makes an X at the wrist with the left hand which also forms a fist — right hand furthest from the body.

59.   Step back to Ride the Tiger
Step back a complete step with your right foot. It settles turned out 45 degrees. Open your palms and draw the left foot back a few inches to rest on the toes and ball of the foot. Your right open palm, facing front, circles out and up to near your right ear and your left palm descends in a curve to brush near your left thigh.

60. Turn Body and Sweep Lotus with Leg

Take both arms out to your left side and make a 360 degree full circle turn to your right on your right leg. Keep your arms horizontal, palms down and turn on your toes. Shift your weight on to your left foot when you complete your circle and take your right foot across to your left and up in a circle so that it brushes past underneath both outstretched palms.

61. Bend the Bow and Shoot the Tiger
Your right leg descends close to your left but not touching the
ground. You step out north-west and gently shift your weight on
to it. As you do this your left palm has come to face in towards your
chest and your right palm has come up close to your right ear.
Form both hands into fists and push out west with the left about
solar plexus height. The right pushes out west too but is held
higher and does not go out so far. The 'holes' formed by the thumb
and index finger of each hand face one another as if they were
holding a curved bow which you were bending.

62. Step forward, Deflect downward, Intercept and Punch
Lift the left foot and step a little way south-east, then repeat
movement 16.

63. Withdraw and Push – repeat posture 17.

64. Cross Hands – repeat posture 18.

65. Conclusion

Draw both hands back in front of the armpits, palms down. Gently lower your palms and slowly straighten your legs but leave your knees loose.

Most people double weight at the Conclusion, that is, weight is evenly distributed on both feet.

Comments

1. Obviously it was not necessary when describing the Short Form to constantly repeat the suggestions made in previous chapters on how to move. This Form is based on the Form made famous by Cheng Man-ch'ing. I could say that it *is* the Cheng Form but only Cheng could do that Form.
2. Once you have 'got' the Form by heart you should go back and revise earlier points.

3. Try each posture as static and dynamic and study how to connect. Search through your body and check each detail. The movement of T'ai Chi is so unusual for us that it is doubtful that we can reach perfection in it. There is always some small or big element missing. However, we can derive consolation from the old saying that it is better to travel than to arrive. We are on our way.

Experiences and Anecdotes

I would like to tell you about some of the variations in the Form through various experiences of mine. It is not useful for you to try them at this stage as you will have your work cut out doing the one Form correctly.

You may remember the Chinese lady who taught me the Wu style. She would not admit that the posture of Single Whip shown in this book was correct, yet thousands of people in China and elsewhere do it that way. In the photograph shown here you will see a Wu style way of Single Whip. Note that the body is inclined but the spine and head are in alignment. In a second variation the trunk is vertical but the feet are double weighted, also Wu style. There is a second style developed in modern China called Combined T'ai Chi Chuan which incorporates several styles in one Long Form. We have Single Whip from that style too. You are learning

Yang style, developed by the Yangs who inherited it from the Chen family. Again we show the Yang Single Whip, though some variations in this are found too. Then there is the style taught by Lien Ying Kuo, now deceased, a master of T'ai Chi, Pakua and Hsing-I. He taught for many years in Portsmouth Square in San Francisco, sometimes known as 'T'ai Chi Park'. His Single Whip may have been influenced by his involvement in the two other internal styles.

You will be familiar by now with the movement of turning in the rear foot at the beginning, during or end of a movement. I was always taught to turn in at the end. But in 1984 I met Master Mantak Chia, who taught people to turn in at the beginning. He it was who also opened up for me the question of the scapula to a much more marked degree than I had done previously. When you become more proficient you can experiment and see which you prefer. There is a strong case for turning in first because you are in a more stable position *before* you move your weight forward. This could be useful in a defence situation. However, it can be argued that a turn in of the foot combined with a turn of the waist and trunk can combine to give added strength to the circularity of a movement. People who study T'ai Chi for a long time reach their own preferences.

Some people, including some of my own former students, do T'ai Chi because they want something aesthetic in the way of exercise. I would sometimes come into a class and students would be training. Often they would be so wrapped up in the delicate hand and arm movements that they would lose their root, their contact with the ground. In T'ai Chi you should always try to be well rooted — your weight and sense of where you are should be *down*. If your imagination begins to run away with you into your aesthetic enjoyment you 'float' upwards in a curious way, and you can easily be pushed off balance. In fact, you *are* off balance. This root needs constantly re-establishing by coming back down to earth. If your attention is easily distracted by other things, whether they are inside you or outside you, then you have lost. Then you must come back to your lower legs and abdomen, empty your arms and upper body and make them light and free; your head should be free and 'rise up'.

If your emotions are agitated then you are certain to have a 'full' chest; instead it needs to be 'empty' so that the breath can flow in and out and the body movements can be free and smooth, relaxed and calm. Remember as a fundamental that T'ai Chi is always concerned with practicalities like always driving on the left side of the road in England and the right side of the road in the USA. If your mind occupies itself with such things then your root will gradually be established. We shall go into this some more in the next chapter.

5

PUSH HANDS TRAINING

'A temporary success secured by irregular means gives him no satis-faction; it is stolen, not honestly come by.'

This quotation from Arthur Waley's *Analects of Confucius* is apt for the beginning of this chapter, because Push Hands Training is where we test whether our understanding of the Form has been 'secured by irregular means' or 'honestly come by'. Push Hands is a traditional part of the art, in which you and a partner alternately use your force and yielding to force as a means of testing your root, your correct alignment, your sinking, relaxation and so forth. When you train alone you are like a monk who lives in a cell alone; whilst he is alone he can feel that he 'loves' the whole world, but if someone calls to see him, and he displeases the monk then the latter may not love any more... When you do push hands you find out if you can relax or not.

The application of the same principle of yielding found in Push Hands has appeared in many aspects of Chinese life and culture. In warfare even, Mao Tse Tung's guerrilla tactics took advantage of it. Mao rarely sent his troops into pitched battles with the invading Japanese army. He let the enemy advance and attack a territory whilst his troops melted and yielded into the countryside, mingling with the peasants. When the initial attack of the enemy had petered out he would press in to the attack, aiming at the weakest point and using his own smaller force at the weakest point. This principle, from the Taoist teachings, set the tone for many succeeding guerrilla groups of different persuasions.

We are working on a much smaller and less belligerent scale. When we train in Push Hands we try to sense the weakness in our partner's balance; whether his centre of gravity is rightly placed and if he is rooted. At the same time we aim to see that when we are pushed we are able to yield and not 'freeze'. This word freeze or if you like petrify is a common fault in everyone at one time or another. When someone is pushed a moment comes when he should be free from the oncoming push, and be ready to counter-push. If he is not aware of this moment he loses himself for a moment, freezes, and goes off balance. This is another of the secrets I spoke about earlier. The fact that I have told you about it will make no difference; you will still freeze until you understand what should be done at that moment.

Push Hands Training is a perfect example of the principle of the Tao, which, like flowing water, always seeks to find a way round, without force. It is like a plant which grows through rock, finding a way, gently, sensitively. Water is softer than rock but indestructible and irresistible. So Push Hands should not be regarded as a contest, though it is hard not to feel a sense of competition rising inside you as you train. If you feel this competitive spirit then concentrate more on the fundamentals of what you are attempting. Try to feel a liking for your partner as another human being; this will help you to relax.

On a day to day level the ramifications of Push Hands may be profound. If we look about us we see that competition, in its widest sense, is what tears human life apart. Competition in civilised society seems to be a necessary component. In Utopia it may not be but we have to look at what we find. This being the case, perhaps we should look for a means to reduce the competition at least in areas where we do have influence. If someone pushes me in Push Hands training I try not to take this as a threat or personal affront; this can be a simple aim. I accept the existence of the other person and his 'right' to push; it is what we are there for after all. So I do not oppose his push either with muscular force or emotional resistance. His push is Yang, active, masculine. My yielding is Yin, negative, feminine. When the Yang and the Yin flow together there is harmony. When aggression and submission meet there is neutrality. So I accept what he is doing and the effect is to soften or neutralise it.

'A soft answer turneth away wrath', is an apt Biblical saying for the case. It is interesting to point out that in books about Chinese philosophy, T'ai Chi, Taoism, Zen and so forth, the Yang and Yin forces are invariably spoken about. They are two forces. Yet the result of their meeting is not given a particular name or prominence. I am talking about some word such as harmony. Yin — Yang — harmony would make three forces. A third force is inevitable when Yin and Yang meet. Yang is modified by Yin and is no longer pure Yang, and Yin is modified by Yang and is no longer pure Yin. At a certain moment, perhaps the moment of 'freeze' for beginners, something different is possible. Then the moment disappears and the possibility is lost, for that moment.

> ...all phenomena, on every scale, from the sub-atomic to the cosmic, are the result of the meeting and interaction of three principles or forces...nothing can happen without the intervention of a third force or principle. If two forces only come together nothing occurs. (Kenneth Walker, *A Study of Gurdjieff's Teaching*, Cape 1957)

In order for you to cultivate your Push Hands and to see its implications for your personal life outside the T'ai Chi training context, it is important to become more aware of constant change. The oldest book in the world, the *I-Ching*, known in English as 'The Book of Changes', was revered by China's best known sage, Confucius. He is said to have wished that he could live for fifty more years in order to study the *I-Ching* for a longer time. So, we cannot aspire to absorb change into our lives overnight, but we are on our way. To absorb it, to be aware of change, we must be awake. To be awake requires an effort. We learn to make some kind of effort throughout T'ai Chi training. My partner pushes and I accept and yield; I absorb his force and so I change; then I in turn push; I change once more and he accepts and changes, so changing me! And so it goes on. If you see yourself freeze, then try to see how to continue to change instead. For this we need a kind of continuous paying of attention to what is going on, like flowing water. This is where the effort lies.

All our vital processes exemplify the idea of change. Our heart beats, our breath goes in and out, our blood and lymph flow, our nervous impulses travel, our food comes in and is utilised, our life itself waxes and wanes. But on our psychological level this rhythm, this continuity is broken into hundreds of small, unco-ordinated pieces.

Let's move on to a practical study of Push Hands.

A. Preliminaries.
    Go back over the earlier sections which dealt with relaxation. Make sure you are clear about the basic stance as in Press or Push postures. Revise the movements of Ward off, Roll-back, Press and Push.

B. Single Push Hands — feet do not move.
    Take up a position with your partner as shown in the photograph with the backs of your right wrists touching lightly, just above the joint in fact. Two-thirds of your weight is on your front leg and a third on the back leg, which is still slightly bent.

1. Your partner, using his rear leg as a drive, gently pushes against your right wrist. His force must come from his leg, not his arm, then through the sacrum, up the spine, through the scapula, then elbow and to the end of the forearm. His body moves as one unit, linking all these different sections.

    You sense his force and yield to it. You are moved only by his force and not by any intentional pulling back of your own. For you to do this your body too must move as a unit, absorbing his energy down to your feet. Principally your rear foot takes it, as your weight is shifted backwards.

    If your partner were to continue to move forward in a straight line and you were to shift weight back, a point would be reached where you could no longer yield and you would begin to topple over or at best lean backwards a long way. To prevent this and divert his force you turn your wrist a little to the right, leading his straight line into a curve. As your body so moves in a unified way

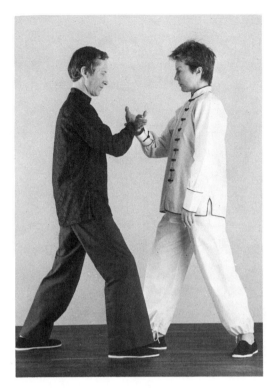 

the effect of your turning your body at the waist automatically takes your wrist, where it is connected to his, into the same curve.

Likewise, if this curve were continued without change it too would lead to a position of strain, so you begin to turn your waist to the right, taking the joined wrists into a circular path. As the circle continues you find yourself applying a force or push to your partner's wrist and it is his turn to yield to you.

You continue to train like this, for a while, moving the wrists from the feet. Keep your wrist movement in a more or less horizontal plane for the moment.

2.   Once you are familiar with the horizontal plane and can yield to some extent then let your partner apply some force in a slight upward direction or a downward direction causing you to yield in that direction yourself and adapt to the new movements involved. You will discover yourself how to keep your body unified and not broken up.

3.   Now carry your yielding an important step further. As your partner pushes forward let your wrist come closer to your body so that in effect he is pushing the palm side of your wrist against your chest. You sense the push on your chest itself. At this point you

yield with your chest by sinking or turning, depending on the direction of this push, and take it round in a circular path, then continue to push forward whilst he in turn yields. Experiment with allowing the push to touch different parts of your body: shoulder, plexus, lower rib cage, and so on. In each case that part of the body yields with the waist turn.

4.   Moving on we now make use of the palm of the hand. Let your partner, instead of resting his wrist against yours, rest the palm of his hand against it, in the same place as before. He repeats the same mode of pushing and you yield, turning your waist to the left and then right. As you reach the point of the circle nearest your body you turn your own palm upwards, and inwards, not losing arm contact with his wrist. He turns his palm into a vertical plane, facing his body, as in the previous exercise with the wrists, and you turn your palm back down and out to rest on his wrist in turn. You continue to push and he yields. Then when your push reaches its maximum distance for him he turns his palm in and down, you turn yours into a vertical plane, and he pushes.

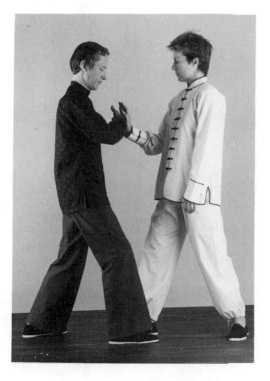 

 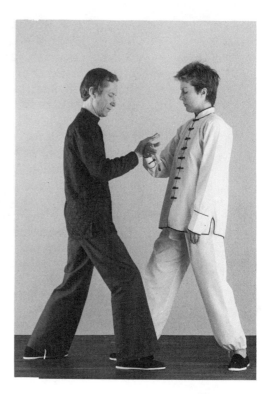

5. Try the same exercises – up to 4. – with the left hand leading and the left foot in front, then the right hand leading and the left leg in front, the left hand leading with the right in front so that you have four different combinations. By training in the different exercises with different combinations of hand and leg positions your body will become more attuned to yielding; more sensitive to giving way from different angles.

When you are accustomed to training in these ways we can move on to the next step which is Double Push Hands.

Double Push Hands

In T'ai Chi we never push with equal force with both hands if it can be avoided. This would be double weighting of the hands. Take up the same relative position with your partner as in Single Push Hands. Right foot is forward. You place your right forearm across your body as in the Ward off posture, with your left palm held behind your right. Your partner rests his right palm on your right wrist and his left palm on your right elbow. Remember to keep your right elbow lowered, not jutting out from the shoulder.

Your partner begins to apply his push as before, with both hands this time. You yield once more and turn your waist. As he comes in close you rest your left palm on his right elbow and turn your right wrist as in 4. Your partner turns his right arm into the Ward off position and his left palm takes up the position behind the right palm. You are now in the pushing role and you move forward with your push, as a unit. In turn your partner yields and the cycle repeats itself. Experiment with this method as you did in the previous one, substituting arms and legs in different relationships.

Push Hands with Roll-back, Withdraw, Push and Press.

We now move on to using particular movements from the Form for different methods of attack and defence. Take up the same relative foot position as before, right foot leading. Your partner rests his hands as in Double Push Hands. As he pushes forward you roll-back to your right, but only about halfway; not to the limit of your balance. With the roll-back movement your left arm points vertically upwards and rests against his advancing right arm, above the elbow. See the photograph for a clearer idea of this. Your right arm remains as before. When your partner finds that his push is diverted by your roll-back movement he turns his right palm in to face his body and slides his left palm to touch it in the Press position.

He continues to press towards the centre of your body. You do not lose contact with his arms but rest your palms on his advancing right arm. You turn your waist and lead his press to your left side. As you do so your left palm slides to his right elbow and your right palm to his right wrist. You turn away to your right and push him back. He in turn does Roll-back, Withdraw, Push and Press and the cycles repeat themselves.

This section is very difficult to put into precise words but with a partner and the photographs to help you you will get it. You can try with the left foot leading, with the left foot and left arm leading, and with the right arm and left foot leading. There are other and

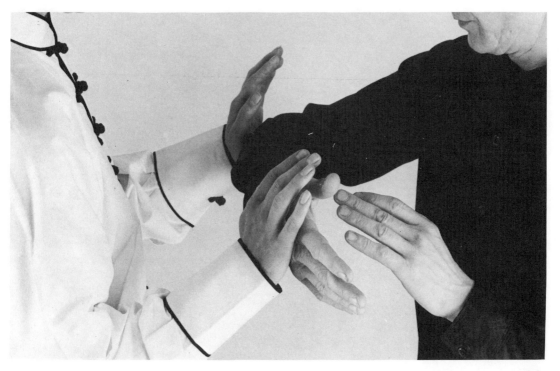

more complex ways of doing Push Hands. But if you become skilled at the methods given in this chapter you will have a firm foundation for future steps.

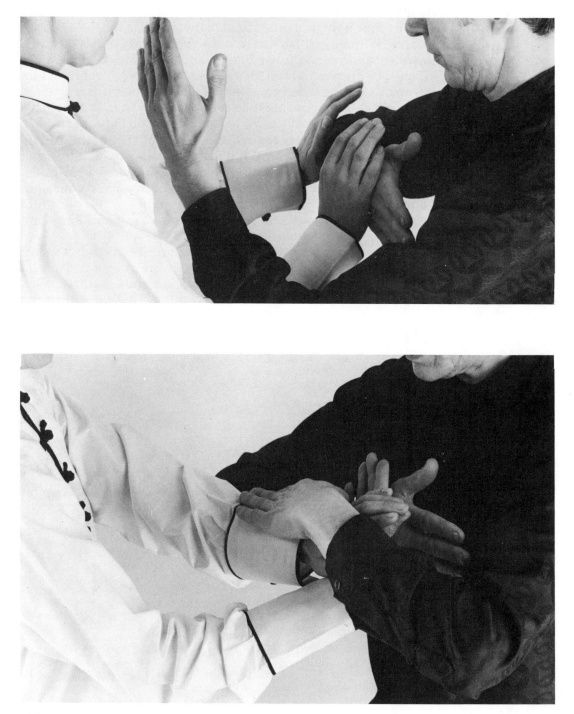

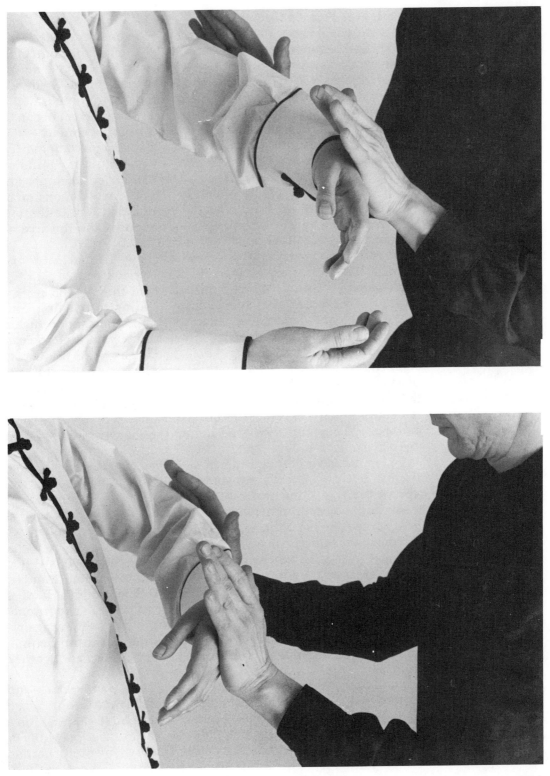

Experiences and Anecdotes

This section will I hope throw more light on the preceding exercises. When I first began to do Push Hands I had no idea of the point of it. My martial arts background of strong physical action gave me no hint of the reason for doing such a soft type of movement. Gradually I realised the purpose behind Push Hands as outlined at the beginning of this chapter, and became aware that when I began to push my intention and force went into the point of contact — my partner's arm. This showed me that I was still wanting a competition, still wanting to 'win'. Then as I slowly began to put my mind or rather my attention into my legs and feet and tried to empty my head, arms and chest of any intention to win, a new dimension of experience opened up. I could see the fluctuations in my attention between my feet and the upper part of my body, and the accompanying rise and fall of tension and relaxation.

When I started to try and pass on to others what I had learned of T'ai Chi it became very clear to me how difficult people find the Push Hands training. When I pushed them they would freeze, usually at the point of changing from yielding to pushing, and they easily lost balance. You cannot push air, you cannot push a silk cloth on a pole, because they are yielding by nature. You can push a frozen silk cloth or a rigid pole. I had to try to get this across and demonstrate it, time and again. Eventually some of the students began to get it. But they lost it within minutes of getting it. I guess that the side of human nature which wants to fight back and resist is so strong that the principles of Push Hands will never become automatic. They will always be something that requires constant vigilance.

You must give your partner just sufficient pressure to push against but not a really substantial surface, otherwise he will uproot the feet from under you. When you push your root or stance must be solid otherwise you will overbalance. You will, to misquote a famous politician, 'become inebriated by the exuberance of your own impetuosity'.

Sometimes, as an experiment and a complete change, it is a good idea to break all the conventions. Take a really tough stance and let your partner give you a really good push. You resist him as hard as you can and just experience the result. Then you can experiment by pushing leg against leg, raised from the ground, pushing against his shoulder from the side, pushing his shoulders from behind, and so on. We often tried such experiments in class and learned from them.

Another variation is to take up the basic Push Hands stance and let two people, one behind the other, push against your raised right arm. Relax your rear leg but fairly straight so that the force travels down your leg but along the bone; the muscles play little or no part. You sink your right scapula and you will be pretty hard to budge. I often have tried this and so have others. We all realised

that as soon as we tried to fight back and resist the push by tensing our muscles the superior force of the two people pushing would topple us over. But provided the force of their push was transmitted through us and down to the ground it was well nigh impossible. This is so because they were trying to push the earth itself away from them.

I once had a very tough, square-built student who had played Rugby Union as a young man. He was very strong but even so wanted to learn this soft art. He brought all the force he had used in passing out tackles in Rugby to bear on the subject of T'ai Chi. As I expected he at first found it a problem; but he was intelligent and open minded and soon was able to relax his considerable muscles and begin to do the Form very competently. When it came to Push Hands though he was at a loss. The notion of yielding to a push is not the principle tactic in Rugby Union and I frequently saw a puzzled look come into his eyes when I stopped him and pointed out that he was pushing or pulling in an unsuitable way. Fortunately for me I was sufficiently skilful to be able to prove my point. He one day asked me to let him really have a go at me and come in as strongly as possible. I agreed and he let me have it; almost a rugby tackle. I yielded and sent him off balance. Even so he did not go down on to the floor. He had short legs, and so a low centre of gravity, with a good root, no doubt cultivated by keeping balance on the games field. He made a lot of progress.

After a while pressure of work made him leave the class. Some months went by and I met him at a friend's house. He told me he had not had time to train, that he had forgotten much of what he had learned, but wanted a book to remind him. I let him have a good book and he thanked me; he said he mainly wanted it to help him relax more.

Not long after that he suffered a heart attack and died. From time to time I have wondered if he had some kind of foreknowledge of his impending fate and was reaching out to T'ai Chi to help him to ward off.

Another student of mine was an attractive actress. She was aesthetically interested in T'ai Chi and she learned fast. She trained regularly and hard. She could do the Form well and exactly.

But in spite of the fact that her Form was so good I never succeeded in conveying to her the Push Hands process. T'ai Chi always remained for her as some kind of magic dance, wafting her into somewhere, I am not sure where. Whenever she was pushed she lost her composure and her balance. Eventually she became interested in other things and left the class. I met her several years later and she told me that she would never forget what she had learned from T'ai Chi. I wonder what it was.

An occasion may arise for you, as it has for me, in which you think that you have no feelings of aggression or competition in relation to your training partner, but he or she undoubtedly has for you. Then it becomes an interesting struggle for you with yourself; not with him. If another person is aggressive it is hard not to be touched by it. You either feel a certain degree of apprehension or you feel aggressive too. Here it is important to empty your mind and focus clearly on the fundamentals. Do not let yourself be drawn into his aggression. Your yielding force must even become strong enough for both of you, so that both his and your aggression are neutralised. If his aggression causes him to severely lose balance you try not to show any pleasure at this but just continue with the training.

I had an experience of this when I was a teenager, before T'ai Chi. It was in the days when I was a Judo enthusiast. Once I turned up at the Judo club and for some reason there was no one else there except another youngster and his big, elder brother. I had been at the club longer than they had and knew more, but the brother was twice my weight and he could never understand why I could throw him and he could not throw me, in freestyle training. The reason was simple. Whenever we fought he more or less threw himself. This particular afternoon we decided to get changed and train, just the three of us. I knew as soon as we went on the mat that the elder brother was out to get me, by hook or by crook. The expression on his face said he was going to pound me into the mat.

We took hold of one another. I always held him very lightly so that I could tell what he was doing and he could not tell what I was going to do. The grip in Judo is very important and you can sense what a man is going to do through your hands.

Try as he might, big brother could not put me down. I threw him a number of times, neck-locked him, choked him, held him down and so forth. Throughout all these events which were emotionally rather than physically traumatic for my opponent I stayed as cool and polite as possible. I knew if I once started to 'slug it out' with him his superior weight would win. I don't remember how we parted that afternoon; I just found the experience of yielding and the accompanying watchfulness on my part were indelibly printed on my memory. On several other occasions when training in both Judo and T'ai Chi I have had the experience of success without 'trying'. When I was a lowly yellow belt or virtual beginner I travelled from Leeds to London, and went to the South London Judo Club. The resident black belt instructor took me on the mat. His skill was of course vastly superior to mine but after a few minutes I floated him down on to the mat with an outer reaping throw. He got up, looking at me and wondering what had happened. I was not quite sure myself.

What these examples from Judo show is that we need to try to have confidence in a new experience. We have our own boundaries of what we feel we can trust and we are reluctant to stray outside them. Within the safe confines of T'ai Chi we have an area of experiment in which we can try to invest in loss. That is, if someone pushes me I will lose nothing really if I let him − for if I lose balance, so what? Perhaps if I am unbalanced a few times I shall learn something. In the realm of interpersonal relationships we are so often trying to push our point of view; I am right. Or we oppose another's point of view; he is wrong. If I can yield a little I gain from my investment. I have my own point of view and then I have his − two points of view. My mind has more to work on.

With a little thought and application the principle of Push Hands can find its way into our daily lives.

T'AI CHI FOR SELF DEFENCE

In this chapter we shall look at a few movements in which the Form and Push Hands could be used for self defence. It would be misleading you if you got the impression that T'ai Chi is a method to adopt if you wish to defend yourself from a mugger or rowdies. It can be used for that purpose but it would require a level of skill which takes years to acquire. To defend yourself and use the principles of the art is beyond the reach of most of us. It is the Cheng Man-ch'ing's of this world — of whom there are very few — who are capable of that. Cheng died some years ago and his staunchest Western advocate, R. W. Smith, wrote of him: 'I have studied many systems of T'ai Chi and have had the opportunity to see in action the leading teachers of Taiwan, Hong Kong and Singapore. None can stand before Cheng.'

On the other hand this does not stop us from investigating the possibilities inherent in T'ai Chi for self defence techniques. Let's look at some.

1.   Distance is very important in self defence. Through your training in Push Hands you will have a much better appreciation of distance. Look at the two people in the photograph. As they stand, neither can reach the other with a punch. This is the closest you want to get to anyone if a brawl seems imminent.

2.   But they are within kicking distance — just. A on the right can reach B to kick his shin or kneecap.

3.   But if he attempts this then B can shift his weight back and draw his front leg from the ground, as in the Gold Cockerel Stands on One Leg technique, and he can then stamp down on the outstretched attacking leg.

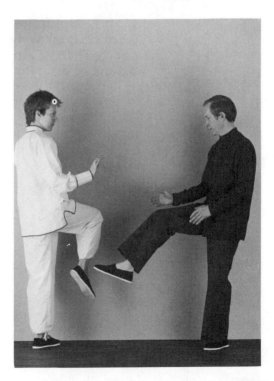

4. If A steps forward with a punch using his right fist to the face, B can shift his weight, roll-back to his right side and deflect the punch. Then he can press the attacking arm down and punch over the top of his own left arm with his right.

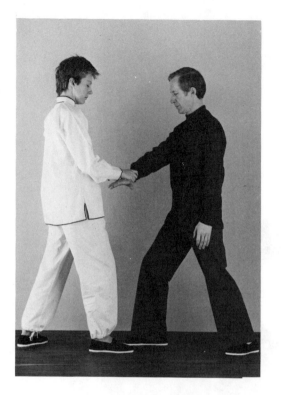

5.   If A grabs B by the right wrist, B places his left hand over it to keep it in place and in turn holds A by the wrist in the same way. As he does so he sinks down, pulling back as in shifting weight. This produces an agonising wrist lock which has to be experienced to be believed. If you try this with a friend, make sure he is a good one. It can be used in any direction: forwards, backwards, sideways and any subdivision of these. Hold firmly, use the whole body as a unit and do not rely solely on muscles.

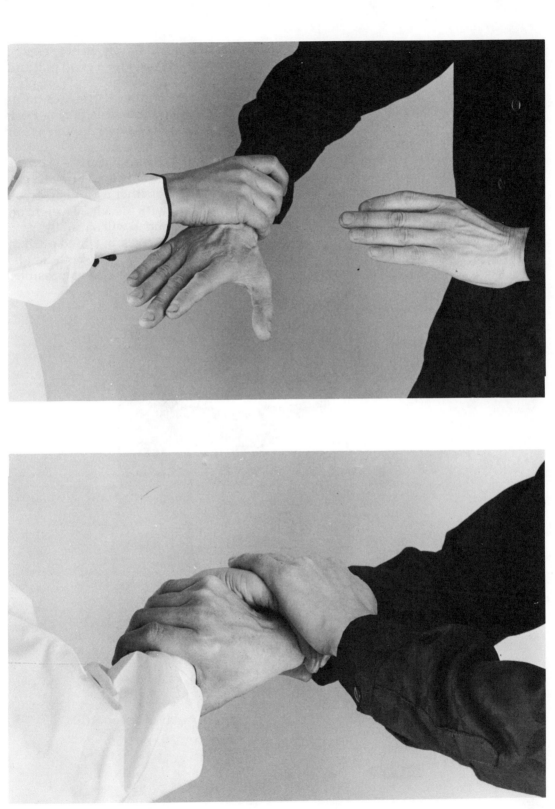

6.   Point of balance is also important. If you simply want to escape from a difficult situation there is a lot to be said for a good pull and push and run. Sometimes it is a good push and pull and run. Or it may be a twist and pull and run. That is why the Push Hands training has such a relevance to self defence because it is during Push Hands that you try to develop the sensitivity to your opponent's or partner's force.

Say that A has been grabbed by B. If A does not want to slam his knee into his attacker's groin but simply wants to get free he can try something else. He brings his hands together up and down on B's arms. At the same time he steps back, with his whole weight on his left leg, sinking, and drawing B with him. B will naturally try to resist this and pull back. When he does, A gives an added push in the same direction and strikes B full in the jaw with both hands, hopefully sending him back. A then runs off as fast as possible.

113

7. Using the Press technique can be useful. If you have a good few months of Push Hands behind you, your forward pushing technique will be much improved. The Press technique is something of a misnomer when it comes to self defence. In fact if you use it 'live' it is sometimes a real shock method.

Say that A has once more been grabbed by the incorrigible B. This time instead of merely pushing him away under the jaw or on the face, A pretends to submit, so that B will be more relaxed and less protected. A puts his hands into the Press position and suddenly strikes B with a jerking movement which begins right down at the feet, remember that, up the spine and through the scapula and elbows exploding into the pressed or even clenched hands. The knuckle of the outside hand can go into the solar plexus region or the face or lower abdomen.

If the attacker has not tensed his abdomen this technique could even kill him. If he has it will wind him. It could break his nose or neck. What I am saying is that you should try it with caution. I merely include it here to show you that T'ai Chi can erupt from calmness into extreme force, like a highly compressed steel spring.

8. Let's look at some of the throwing potential of T'ai Chi. Say that B once more attacks. He is grabbing or punching as usual. A is with his right leg forward and he rolls-back to his outside using his raised left arm. His right arm is ready as shown in the photograph. As he does his roll-back, he steps forward on to his left leg, puts his right palm under B's jaw and his left palm into the small of his back. If you think about it this is like the Ward Off position for the hands, modified by the application. He can either push B down by pushing with his right hand and pressing back with the left or he can help by sweeping with the right leg also, sending B crashing down.

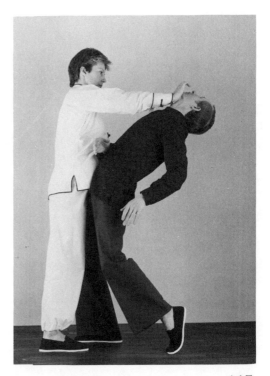

9.   Because of the training you have had in taking weight on one leg it should be easy for you to kick. Remember the Separate Right and Left Foot techniques? Say you are once more confronted by the ever belligerent B whose appetite for unrequited violence is insatiable.

Your weight is on your front leg. Before B moves or as he moves you can sneak your rear leg forward and kick his shin with it. Or if most weight is on your rear leg you can kick him with the front foot. What I am saying is that if your T'ai Chi has been working for you then you will be able to move from a more relaxed to a full-action state more quickly and without giving a lot of warning signals to an aggressor. Your action will be more like that of a snake, which, from the point of view of must of us, seems to strike without warning.

10.   Let's have a look at Shoulder Stroke. Here comes B again. This time he is more subtle and is coming up diagonally from your right rear. As he grabs you, you step round with your right foot to meet him, your right elbow goes into his solar plexus, your left hand may be raised to protect your face and then you swing your right hand down and forward into his groin. If you are feeling desperate you can grab him there until he submits. This may not look like Shoulder Stroke but just use your imagination and you will see it.

11.   With all your training in shifting weight your balance should
have improved. This can only help your technique. B comes again.
As he does so you throw your hands up towards his face to take his
attention away from his feet. Slide your left leg diagonally in from
the side so that the shin bone of your leg touches the side of his
right. Your instep touches his heel. Then just kneel down on your
left leg. He cannot move his leg away and goes down.

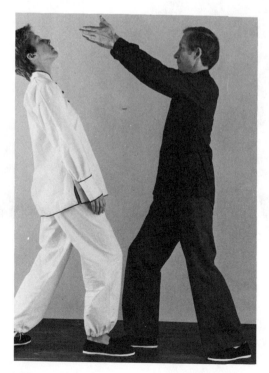 

12.   Finally we come to what I call a whirlwind technique. This is the Cross Hands movement. It is very much a set piece as presented here but you can use all or some of it, depending on the circumstances.

B throws a punch. Your circling right hand deflects it. He kicks and your circling left hand deflects it. As you deflect raise his kicking leg, bring your right hand down and under the leg to strike the testicles. This nasty jolt will probably stop B from seeing the left hand chop which is coming immediately from your left hand which has let go of his leg. Then follow up with a right punch to the jaw or nose. Then follow up with a left to the chest. Groin, neck, jaw, solar plexus. The point about Cross Hands is that contrary circles of the left and right hands combined with the rapid shifting of weight and waist turns have a winding up effect, like the loading of a spring, especially noticeable when done at speed. This wind up can be released in a series of techniques of which I have given only a sample.

This ends our glance at application to self defence. If you stay cool and experiment with a partner you can discover many more such methods. The important thing to remember is not to get flustered. Force not fluster is the watchword, no matter how great or small the force or the potential fluster.

Let's look at a more peaceful scene.

7

T'AI CHI AND OTHER ARTS

You will have gathered that we are very interested in Form in T'ai Chi. We say that correct Form is the basis of everything else and that this correct Form is reached through relaxation and body alignment. It is a fair claim that in general Western people are not avidly interested in Form in the sense used in T'ai Chi. We are interested in the body's attractiveness, its shapeliness, its skin surface, and so on. But this interest is mostly superficial, cosmetic. The Form or posture of a person's body takes second place to his tan, clothes, muscles, or the size of her breasts or the success of her make-up.

Yet in many Eastern countries the posture and deportment of the body was, and to some extent still is, regarded as significant. The notion that a man or woman could have a thoroughly untrained or undisciplined body and still be wise, integrated, mature or whatever superlative you wish to apply, is foreign and incomprehensible over there.

One reason for this must surely be that until the twentieth century most Eastern societies were still traditional. By that I mean that there was a certain unity underlying the daily life. Unity comes from different aspects of the society being related — nothing exists on its own, cut off from the rest. As with society, so with the individual member of that society. For him also to be unified his body, feeling and his thought must be related. As such, a man in whom such a relationship existed was regarded as being someone worth listening to. Yet we in the West do not recognise these signs, and instead look to our media 'stars', with their demoralised lifestyles, for indications as to how we should behave.

I am digressing a little into this slightly moral tone because I hope that you will try to relate your study of T'ai Chi to a wider area of your life, and suggest in this chapter a few avenues of further exploration.

Calligraphy and Painting

In his book, *A First Zen Reader*, Trevor Legget gives an illustration of some Japanese brushwork. It is by a master, and beside it is an illustration of a pupil's work. Legget says that if the motive for making the brush strokes is not pure, if there is a desire for profit or self advancement, then this will show in the finished result. He points out that in the copy of the master's work by the pupil there are weaknesses whose causes we can only guess at but whose existence betrays the state of mind of the pupil.

When we take a posture in T'ai Chi or make a series of movements, or even stand still waiting to begin, we cannot avoid 'painting' our inner state, be it impatience, confusion, peace. It must be the case that when a master calligrapher makes a brush stroke then the more unified he is within himself so it will show in the ink or paint. In T'ai Chi no single part of the body should move on its own. Even when we stand still the relaxation and tension should be evenly spread through the body. This cannot be reached quickly but it is an aim for us.

To move in this direction we need to become more critical of ourselves. We cannot look at the finished product as a painter can, as there is nothing to see, but we can become more aware of our posture and how we move. If we also notice our posture in daily life we can be reminded of our more relaxed state reached during T'ai Chi training and this may help us to relate the two more closely. Just as the brush strokes cited by Trevor Legget indicated the motive, mood, or emotion of the artist so we may find that our posture and movement is very much influenced by our mood or motive. We shall also discover that by influencing our posture we can also influence our mood. The two are related but in most of us this is entirely unconscious; no intentional relationship is aimed at.

Fritz van Briessen wrote a book called *The Way of the Brush*. It is about the painting techniques of China and Japan. From our point of view he said some very interesting things in it. He suggested that in Western eyes the *techniques* of Chinese and Japanese painting are considered of secondary importance, and the *idea* of primary importance. Having swept this misconception aside he states that, 'Chinese painting reaches its culmination in absolute identity of idea and technique.' Whilst we may not be able to appreciate the meaning of this statement we can still learn from it. It once more illustrates what we have been thinking about unity. If our technique in T'ai Chi is correct, our Form will be correct, and this will only be possible if our thought, our mind, our 'i' (mind) is correct.

A Chinese emperor asked a painter to paint a landscape on the wall of the palace. The centre piece of the painting was a cave. When he had finished the work the painter showed it to the emperor and then promptly walked into the cave and disappeared. Finally the painting itself disappeared.

Van Briessen goes on to say that if we wish to understand Chinese painting then we must study the technique and its significance as well as the finished composition. In this way we shall better understand what are commonly regarded as opposites: 'material appearance and spiritual essence'.

Gesture

In Eastern art and religion we find a word, *mudra*. In painting and sculpture we see representations of gods and enlightened beings such as the Buddha making a range of gestures with the hands, arms and feet. These are the mudras. Opinions of scholars vary on the origins of the mudras themselves and of the origins of the word.

Mudras which appear in Buddhist art are said to relate to esoteric

ceremonies or to evoke specific episodes in the life of the Buddha himself. In the Tantric school of Buddhism which spread to China and Japan, the right hand was the Yang or masculine side and the left hand the Yin or feminine side. (In Japan Tantrism is found in the Shingon sect.) The gesture or mudra, among living Buddhists, was often accompanied by a sound or mantra. The mudra sealed or exemplified or was the living expression of the mantra, and the mantra was an audible expression of an idea or powerful thought. Each symbol of a mantra could be a symbol of a colour. For instance the famous 'Om Mani Padme Hum' of Tibet, consisting of six syllables, represented the colours white, blue, yellow, green, red and black. The words themselves mean, 'Ah, the jewel is in the lotus', a saying related to the symbolism of Buddhist meditation.

In making such a gesture or mudra the man was expressing himself completely at that moment. He was unified within himself. This is possibly one of the highest expressions of human understanding in bodily terms, and we are not aspiring to perform it ourselves just yet. I am bringing it to your attention because it emphasises once more the importance of moving in the direction of unity through T'ai Chi in our daily lives.

The inner work required to perform a mudra in the way indicated above is great. But we ourselves can begin by examining our gesture and posture in our lives, in our T'ai Chi, and noting at first the completely disjointed and disorganised state which we find ourselves in. The relatively unified way in which we try to move in T'ai Chi can be a mirror which we hold up to the way in which we usually sit, shave, walk, talk, stand, eat, and so forth. We shall see in this mirror that we have a long way to go. But that does not matter; we are on our way.

T'ai Chi to Music
Sometimes, to try to produce more relaxation in the students in the class, I used to play music on records whilst they were doing the Form. It was very effective.

When you ask people to relax they often try too hard, and become tense. But if you find a suitable piece of music and simply suggest that they move in accordance with the mood of the music they will relax more spontaneously. My favourite piece of music for this purpose is called 'A Bell Ringing in the Empty Sky', played by Goro Yamaguchi in the Explorer series of Nonesuch Records. The music has no rhythm in the commonly accepted sense and is full of peace and inspiration. It has no catchy phrases to distract the mind and it would be first choice.

The rise and fall of volume and pitch and the breathing of the flautist suggests a similar rise and fall to the T'ai Chi student and cannot fail to make a suitable impression.

If you do not like it or cannot get a copy then there are other pieces to choose from. Persian flute music is very beautiful and has

a suitable meditative mood. It is up to you to choose for yourself but I recommend that you do not use rhythmic music at first as this tends to dictate your speed of movement too much. Once you have your music, you try the Form and listen to the music at the same time. As you move you let the mood of the music penetrate into your joints and flesh, taking away tension and haste, and gradually loosening your breath.

When the music stops you will feel it. Something will be missing. It is not just a sound but the whole mood which it inspired. You carry on with the Form then and see if you can still move in the same way without the support of the musical mood. The music suggests something to you of the ever changing Tao, of being in accord. It is up to you to search for that same feeling about life, about yourself, which the music gave you.

T'ai Chi does have feeling; it is only with the right feeling, ultimately, about life and yourself, that you will be able to do it. Cheng Man-ch'ing was a master of the Five Excellences — painting, calligraphy, poetry, medicine and T'ai Chi. I have no doubt that each of these accomplishments helped the others.

Find the music which suits you and use it to help your T'ai Chi. Use your T'ai Chi to help yourself.

Symmetry

Perfect symmetry, in a technical sense, means that if we divide a structure or surface into two halves they will be identical. A circle is symmetrical, for instance, and so is a sphere. In nature, I believe, there is no perfect symmetry. But a further definition from the Oxford dictionary says that symmetry is the 'beauty resulting from right proportion between the parts of a body and any whole...' Early Buddhist art was influenced by Greek art, and it was this second definition of symmetry which applied to it. If you mentally divide a Buddhist statue into two you will not have perfect symmetry, but somehow the balance between the parts of the statue, their proportion, is so 'right' that it can be described as symmetrical.

In T'ai Chi movement we aim for symmetry also, in this second sense. Obviously it once again relates to correct Form, and once again reflects our mental state. The impression given by some Buddhist statues is one of peace, wisdom, presence — it is indefinable. But the cause of this impression is of course directly related to the symmetry, the proportion. If the arm of such a statue were say 10 degrees more to the left, or the head were tilted more to the right, then something would be 'wrong'. We could perfectly well say that the symmetry has been lost. In T'ai Chi when a limb is out of alignment the symmetry has been lost and it means that the awareness of what he is doing has been lost by the performer.

But let us say that in the case of the Buddhist statue the arm was 10 degrees to the left, this 'error' could be alleviated if all the rest of the statue were modified. Of course in a carved stone figure this is impossible but in a human being it is not. This point relates to the saying in T'ai Chi that we never move one part of the body by itself; the body moves as a whole. Suppose you shift your weight forward, extending your rear leg. If you lose track of what you are doing you may tilt your trunk, losing your alignment. If you were at that momemt petrified and became a statue, your Form would never grace the Victoria and Albert Museum. But you can rectify this by bending your rear leg, and bringing your trunk back into vertical.

Coming once more back to our daily lives, and our posture, we find that we are often not symmetrical, either in thought, feeling or action. If you look around you in a bus queue you see a collection of people who, more often than not, are standing, lounging or slouching in most asymmetrical ways. Many of our emotions and thoughts are selfish, conceited or egotistical. They are one-sided, lop-sided. I want more pay but I don't want to work for it. I want her to love me but I won't put myself out for her. There is no symmetry, no balance, no harmony of Yin and Yang in this. If our thoughts and emotions were embodied in the DNA of our genetic make-up then our bodies would be more reminiscent of satirical

cartoons of politicians than the ones we now possess. It is the asymmetrical portrayals by cartoonists which graphically illustrate the points I am trying to make.

Lack of Relationship

In the West today we are bombarded by many teachers of Yoga, Shiatsu, Acutheraphy, Karate, dance, and so on. Unfortunately many of these teachings omit important points such as the ones I have made in this chapter. Advertisements for such teachings call on the urge to be fit, to be healthy, to be beautiful, and forget that most of these arts were descended from a Way or Tao of some kind, to feed man's religious impulse. In travelling West the connection with the root has been cut. Fitness, health and beauty *may* result from following such a teaching in its original form, but these are by-products and not the aim. So we have a situation where a discipline such as Yoga, which means Union with a Supreme Being, is reduced to a method of reducing weight... It is quite a slide down the scale.

What needs to be found or restored in all these things is the relationship between the art being taught and other sides of a man's being. Fortunately for all of us, there are some people in the West working in that direction, trying to understand this relationship in a new way. In the meantime, fingers pointing to the moon, such as T'ai Chi, are still around to remind us of its potential existence.

8 T'AI CHI FOR HEALTH AND SANITY

Robert W. Smith wrote that whoever does T'ai Chi correctly and regularly, twice a day, will, over a period of time, gain the pliability of a child combined with the strength of a lumberjack. He will also reach the peace of mind of a sage. These are the claims of the Chinese.

I cannot endorse these rather far-reaching claims myself, but can say that if you do as Smith says then sometimes you will experience the pliability of a child, sometimes you will experience the strength of a lumberjack and sometimes an unusually deep degree of peacefulness. How long these experiences last, and how often you have them depends on you.

In 1982 an account of Cheng Man-ch'ing's T'ai Chi experiences and some autobiographical passages were published in the USA. They made interesting reading. In the beginning of his life, Cheng suffered from beriberi and rheumatism and was unable to find a cure. He took up some ancient Chinese physical exercises and his health improved. Then he contracted tuberculosis which in those days was often fatal. He began to spit blood and the prognosis was not good.

Someone introduced him to T'ai Chi and his health improved. But after a little while he abandoned the art and suffered a relapse. From then on he never let a day go by without performing his T'ai Chi. His health once more improved and gradually he became famous as a master. His attitude towards himself in his own writings is typically self effacing, but his actions spoke louder than his words. In Push Hands everyone acknowledged that he was invincible. Even so he said that he did not aspire to 'transform his disposition' though it was said that in T'ai Chi such a transformation of character was possible. He said that he could not be a living proof of this but would leave it to someone 'more highly evolved' than himself to do so.

In 1980, Jou Tsung Hwa wrote a book which claimed that Cheng liked wine too much for his own good; that this had led to his premature death from a heart attack at the age of 74. The year was 1975. I mention this here for two reasons. The first is to criticise the writer because he had been a guest of Cheng's in the latter's home, called him 'Master' though he was not his formal student, and looked up to him as a T'ai Chi man. For these three reasons he should not have written in such a way about him. Also, since Cheng is dead he cannot reply, should he even have deigned to do so.

But, given that these statements have been made we can remind ourselves that Cheng himself said that he was not able to transform his disposition through T'ai Chi. If he loved wine and the effects of wine, then it was part of his disposition.

Jou Tsung Hwa himself, at the age of 47, became ill with an enlarged heart and gastroptosis. The year was 1964. His doctor did not give a very favourable prognosis but a friend introduced him to a vigorous T'ai Chi master. Within a few weeks he began to improve daily and after about three years his stomach was cured. Since then he trained without missing a day.

What can we say though about the benefits of T'ai Chi training for our own health? I think everyone would agree that we need some form of exercise if our daily work or hobbies do not give it to us. A modern man can spend all day in an office, responding to phone calls, to his secretary and colleagues, customers and friends, and hardly use his body at all. He can travel home in a car or slumped on a train seat and then sit in front of a television set until bedtime. He may jog or play squash but these exercises can be harmful as any doctor will tell you. Torn knee ligaments, foot and ankle injuries and other ills have befallen hundreds of people who took up these pastimes. Fatigue and tension often result from competitive sports with large quantities of lactic acid being produced. I do not knock these things wilfully, but point them out because T'ai Chi has none of their disadvantages and can be done at any time in a relatively small space and with no special equipment.

T'ai Chi does not accelerate the heart, on the contrary it can even slow it down; it co-ordinates the mind and body and even calms the emotions. It uses all the joints of the body, gently, stretches the muscles and tendons and keeps them in good shape, and gives the human being a holiday from his usual self.

Claims have been made about the efficacy of T'ai Chi in curing various ills which range from obesity to high blood pressure, glandular disorders to tuberculosis. More cautious commentators say that it can help in such conditions but that other factors need to be taken into account also. One thing is certain, however, that T'ai Chi keeps a person's body in better shape than neglect. We all know that the population of the world is growing and the increasing number of elderly people is a big burden on the health and social services. For us in England this is a serious problem and the wards of geriatric patients are expanding by leaps and bounds. I would suggest that programmes of exercise such as T'ai Chi be encouraged among the middle-aged to elderly to try to keep them mobile for as long as possible. We need much more prevention before we are obliged to look for a cure.

Oriental ideas about health and medicine differ from ours, traditionally. One of the differences is in the view of the doctor and patient relationship. We go to a doctor when we are ill. In China you go to your doctor to keep well. Your doctor fails if you fall ill. We need to take a leaf from this book and prevent people from becoming ill and then having to resort to expensive drugs to get better. Our medical programmes should be geared to prevention. In China and in emigrant and second and third generation Chinese communities the world over, many people train at T'ai Chi in the mornings in open spaces. I have no statistics, but if they are there, and if we could compare with our own, we would probably find that people stay much more healthy and active into old age in China than in England.

We have all probably seen on television how Japanese factory workers and office workers go through set routines of exercise at work. I am not suggesting that we coerce the independently minded British to do such a thing; we would have a strike on our hands. But such training could be made available. In the USA the study of T'ai Chi as a therapy is increasing. Since we often imitate the Americans we may yet see the whole of Hyde Park thronged with metropolitan denizens at six thirty in the morning, doing their T'ai Chi.

Yearning K. Chen, writing in Shanghai in 1947, claimed that he had cured many people of anaemia, gastro-enteritic diseases, high blood pressure and primary tuberculosis using T'ai Chi. His book on the subject was a bestseller and found wide acceptance in the West when it was first published in English.

Master T. T. Liang, a contemporary of Cheng Man-ch'ing, took up T'ai Chi for his health. He was seriously ill, he does not say from what, and trained very seriously to cure himself. When he got better he went into other sides of the art and carried on his study for more than thirty years. As I have lost touch with his movements, I last heard he was back in Taiwan — I do not know if he is still on this earth.

Douglas Lee, a Chinese born in Canada, is a kidney transplant technician. He has taught T'ai Chi in several places in the USA and Canada and recommends that it is an exercise very suitable for elderly people as well as the young. Perhaps because of his scientific background and connection with Western medicine, he makes smaller claims for the benefits of the art. He says it can be useful for people with 'psychosomatic illnesses and hypertension'.

Yang Ming-shih was born in China in 1924 and later emigrated to Japan. He is a Karate man as well as a T'ai Chi teacher. Among the claims he makes for T'ai Chi are an improvement in digestion, strengthening of the abdominal muscles, improvement in blood circulation and reduction in ulcer problems, relaxation, weight reduction, amelioration of haemorrhoids and overall body improvement. In the martial arts fraternity Yang is best known as a T'ai Chi instructor to some of the leading Karate men in the world.

Dr Tseng Ju-pai (Chiu Yen), author of *Primordial Pugilism — T'ai Chi Chuan*, suffered from stomach problems caused by a heavy workload. He met the famous pupil of the renowned Yang Cheng-fu, Chen Wei Ming, who advised him to take up the art. Chen himself had been very ill some twenty years earlier and had gained good health through learning from Yang. Dr Tseng was encouraged by this and began to train assiduously. Soon his health too improved. A friend of mine met him in Hong Kong when he was very advanced in years and reported that he was in good health and still able to perform all the T'ai Chi weapons Forms, smoothly and with perfectly free joints. Dr Tseng also wrote a book on the weapons of the art.

Chia Siew Pang of Singapore is another T'ai Chi teacher, and he says that the art is particularly beneficial to the cardio-pulmonary system. He claims that 'a half an hour T'ai Chi workout would be equivalent to the exercise benefit derived from a three hour game of golf'. So it is certainly a timesaver. He also advises one to refrain from training when suffering from acute illnesses such as influenza.

Tang Mon Hun is a Wu style T'ai Chi man and does not disagree with his Yang style brothers about the benefits to health. Rheumatism, chronic indigestion, mental fatigue, insomnia and chronic arthritis are among the ills he gives as improved through training.

To complete this brief catalogue of testimonials we can cite our only woman Master of T'ai Chi, Madame Bow Sim Mark, whom I had the privilege of meeting in 1984 when she visited England. She is particularly famous for her mastery of the Wudang Sword and runs the Chinese Wushu Research Institute in Boston, USA. Among the benefits she lists are: regulation of the neuro system, promotion of the circulatory system, massage of the internal organs, strengthening of the skeletal structure and balance of hormone production. She herself is no longer young but can leave most who are far behind in matters of lithe body movement, flexibility, energy and vitality.

But let us leave the last word to the Chinese in China. In 1980 Professor Qu Mianyu wrote the following piece. (Note that we are following the modern Chinese romanisation of their language.)

Taijiquan (T'ai Chi Chuan) is a branch of the traditional sport of Wushu. As a means of keeping fit and preventing and curing diseases it has been widely practised among the people since the 16th century. Its popularity has further increased with the adoption of a simplified set of exercises in 1956. Forming an important part of the treatment often prescribed in hospitals and sanitoriums, Taijiquan has proved its efficacy in treating chronic diseases such as high blood pressure, neurasthenia and pulmonary tuberculosis.

The salutary effects of Taijiquan have much to do with its characteristic features, namely: 1. the exercises require a high degree of concentration, with the mind free from distractions; 2. the movements are slow and uninterrupted like a flowing stream; and 3. breathing is natural, sometimes involving abdominal respiration, and is performed in rhythmic harmony with body movements. From the point of view of sports medicine these characteristics are important factors contributing to the prevention and treatment of diseases.

The high degree of concentration required in the Taijiquan exercises also benefits the function of the central nervous system. Training the mind and body at the same time these exercises stimulate the cerebral cortex, causing excitation in certain regions and protective inhibitions in others. This enables the cerebrum to rest and relieves the cerebral cortex of the pathological excitation caused by ailments, thus helping to cure certain nervous and mental diseases.

The results of recently completed testing and examination involving Taijiquan practitioners are of particular interest to medical and sport personnel. In the project, healthy subjects aged 50 to 89 were divided into two groups and given a battery of tests. Group 'A' consisted of 32 persons who practised Taijiquan regularly while Group 'B' or Control Group was composed of 56 individuals who did not engage in Taijiquan training. In general those in Group 'A' were found to have a stronger physique, characterised by more efficiently functioning cardiovascular, respiratory, osseous and metabolic systems.

Specific Findings

In regard to cardiovascular efficiency, the two groups underwent a functional test of stepping up and down a 40cm. high bench 15 times within a minute. All but one person in Group 'A' could bear this workload with normal type responses in blood pressure and pulses. In the control group, however, capability of bearing this workload decreased and abnormal responses (such as type of step reaction and dystonia reaction) increased with the age of the subjects. The difference was also evident in electrocardiograms. Abnormal patterns such as the prolongation of the P-R interval, the complex QRS and the QT duration, the reduction of the RV5 amplitude, the depression of the ST and the inversion of T, were found in 28.2% of the subjects in Group 'A' and 41.3% in Group 'B'.

These findings suggest that regular practice of Taijiquan results in an increased supply of blood to the coronary arteries, more forceful heart contractions and improved hemodynamic processes. Moreover, Taijiquan may enhance the regulatory function of the central nervous system, improve the coordination of the various organs of the human body, increase the tension of the vagus nerves, ensure adequate supplies of blood and oxygen to the tissues of the various organs and facilitate substance metabolism — all of which contribute to a lower rate of incidence of hypertension and arteriosclerosis. The average blood pressure was 134.1/80.8 mmHg. for Group 'A' and 154.5/82.7 mmHg. for group 'B', while the rate of incidence of arteriosclerosis was 39.5 and 46.4% respectively. Regular practice of Taijiquan exercises can increase the elasticity of the lung tissues, the respiratory magnitude of the chest (which helps retard the ossification of the rib cartilages), ventilatory capacity of the lungs and improves the exchange of oxygen and carbon dioxide. Experiments showed Group 'A' to be superior in both the respiratory discrepancy of the chest and vital capacity. The greater vital capacity results from a stronger diaphragm and muscles of the thoracic walls, greater lung tissue elasticity and a lower rate of ossification of the rib cartilage. For those whose breathing is already limited by ossification of rib cartilages, abdominal respiration accompanying Taijiquan exercises will help ventilation of the lungs and, through rhythmic change of abdominal pressure, speed up blood flow and gas exchange in the alveoli pulmonum. This explains why, when completing the functional test, Group 'A' subjects breathed more easily and recovered more quickly than those in the control group.

Taijiquan exercises can also strengthen the bones, muscles and joints. Take the spine for instance. Since many Taijiquan movements hinge on the waist and involve a great deal of lumbar movement, systematic exercise can be beneficial to the form and structure of the lumbar vertebral and indeed the spinal column as a whole. Researchers noted that only 25.8% of the subjects in Group 'A' suffered from spinal column deformities whereas in the control group the percentage was 47.2%. Furthermore, fewer Group 'A' subjects were the victims of common, age-related hunchback deformities. Individuals in this group had more flexible spines, as evidenced by the fact that 77.4% of them were able to do touch-toes, as against 16.6% in the control group. X-ray examination indicated that the rate of incidence of senile osteoporosis was 36.6% for Group 'A' and 63.8% for Group 'B'. Senile osteoporosis, which often leads to deformity and inflexibility of joints, is degenerative and mainly caused by inactivity of the osteoblasts resulting in their inability to produce sufficient matrices so that more bone is resorbed than formed. It may also be caused by such factors as reduced blood supply to bones owing to arteriosclerosis and poor absorption of calcium and potassium from food, due to lack of hydrochloric acid in the gastric juices. Insofar as Taijiquan can prevent or lessen such disorders, its role in retarding the ageing process is noteworthy.

Limited data were uncovered relative to the effects of Taijiquan exercises on substance metabolism in the human body. However, judging from the differences between the two groups of oldsters in skeletal changes and in the incidence of arteriosclerosis the beneficial effects of exercise appear significant as far as the metabolism of fats, proteins and calcium and potassium salts is concerned. In recent years, several researchers in other countries have studied the role of physical exercises in

delaying senescence. Cholesterol levels have dropped sub-
stantially for those engaged in regular exercises. Experiments
conducted on elderly people afflicted with arteriosclerosis
reveal that after five or six months training there has been an
increase of albumin and a marked decrease of globulin and
cholesterol in their blood, while symptoms of arteriosclerosis
have greatly diminished.

Conclusion
These findings, though preliminary and superficial, suggest
that a regular programme of Taijiquan exercises can be of
benefit to one's physical well-being.

9

THE 'CHI' OF T'AI CHI

I cannot help referring to my favourite martial arts writer, Robert Smith, again, as I begin this chapter. He wrote that most English writers on the subject of *chi* maintained an 'embarrassed silence'. I will step away from this embarrassed Anglo-Saxon flock and speak, though I may be laughed to scorn by them.

Chi and its meaning are only difficult because we make them so. I have been interested in such subjects for over thirty years and met many like-minded people; I do not feel that because I am English and not Chinese that I should not open my mouth. Chi is energy. It can be experienced, just as some other energies can be. When we are frightened our energy level for action or flight rises; the same in anger, haste or any strong emotional reaction. If we read a medical book it tells us that this is the adrenalin released into our blood stream. But this is simply a medical term for a process. Men and women experienced this reaction long before the application of 'adrenalin flow' to this experience. Our difficulty, if we need to talk about chi, is to identify which, of the many energies flowing in and out of the human body, is the one or ones which we call chi. Is there in fact only one chi?

As laymen let's look at the different sources of experience we have of our bodies. There are heartbeat and blood flow, breath and oxygen intake and expulsion of carbon dioxide, intake and digestion of nourishing food and the resulting comforting effects or indigestion, weakness from various illnesses, well being from sleep, fatigue from physical and mental work, exhaustion, hunger, thirst, sexual desire and fulfilment or frustration − the list is far from complete. All these experiences and the sensations and feelings accompanying them come from a complex series of processes. It would need a very special human being to be able to identify exactly which sensation was caused by which process, since their interconnectedness is very great.

Most people have experienced sexual desire, but what is sexual desire? Thousands of writers, even some English ones, have not maintained an embarrassed silence on that topic... But if we asked those same writers what sexual desire is, how many could answer? What makes the books of these writers comprehensible is that we have a common experience of the subject and this makes us able to understand what the writer is saying. But in trying to identify the experience can we say that it is blood flowing into a sexual area, is it increased oxygen supply, is it nervous energy, or simply the secretions of the sexual glands? We don't know the answer but we do know the experience.

Chi is one of the cornerstones of Oriental medical thinking. Practitioners of acupuncture, acupressure, herbal remedies, moxibustion and anaesthesia, which have been demonstrated to millions of television viewers the world over, make use of the concept of chi to explain their results. When the flow of chi is blocked the organs of the body are not supplied with the energy they need and illness results. All over the human body are invisible meridians or rather channels, to give the correct translation. They are compared to the meridians which cover a globe or map of the world. The chi or vital energy flows along the meridians, just as nervous impulses flow along nerves, and blood along arteries and veins. There can be too much chi or too little chi. Or, there can be the optimum amount, which means that a person is healthy. Western science does not wholeheartedly, or should I say wholeheadedly, accept this. The facts are, though, that Chinese physicians have been using this 'unproven' system on an empirical basis for several thousand years.

Let us take a brief look at some of the things they say.

We spoke earlier about the two forces, Yin and Yang, whose interplay is said to maintain all creation. Yin can be described as a negative force and Yang as a positive. We are all familiar with the positive and negative ends of a battery in a torch or portable radio. When the circuit is switched on the current flows from one pole to the other and the heat of resistance results in light from the filament. As soon as the potential energy in the battery has been used up the bulb no longer works because the current has ceased to flow. There are in fact three phenomena here: positive, negative and light.

Chinese medicine and philosophy say that when the Yin and Yang forces are balanced there is health. Imbalance results in illness.

The symbol which represents the Yin Yang idea is shown here.

It is a symbol which is called the T'ai Chi, meaning Supreme Ultimate. T'ai Chi Chuan means Supreme Ultimate Martial Art Way or Fist. The T'ai Chi we are studying, therefore, is part of Chinese medicine and philosophy and that in turn is part of a much greater scheme known as Taoism and it pre-dates the Indian and Confucian influences in Chinese history by hundreds if not thousands of years. The symbol is black and white with a spot of white in the black and a spot of black in the white. This indicates that nothing in creation is ever completely Yang or completely Yin. Yang is white and Yin is black. There is always a trace of the opposite present.

Some people liken the two black and white shapes of the symbol to two fishes, clinging together like two lovers. You will see that the 'tail' of each fish narrows to a point, signifying that as the Yang or Yin increases the Yin or Yang diminishes. Turning to the human being we find Chinese medicine proposes five Fundamental Substances with it: chi, blood, ching, shen and fluids. If we were to ask a Chinese doctor to define these substances he would not be very interested. His medicine is based on empirical diagnosis and treatment. He examines the patient and observes the signs of the activities of the Fundamental Substances and treats accordingly. He observes that this method works and is sufficient. Can we accept this?

If you went to such a doctor and asked his opinion he would examine your appearance and take your pulse. There is more than one pulse in Chinese medicine because the major organs all make their presence felt in the one pulse which you and I feel at our wrist. His sensitive fingers would tell him whether your pulse was too Yang or too Yin based to a large extent on the chi flow there. This is an over-simplification but it makes the point. He would be able to tell also which organ was not working properly and would treat you to sedate or stimulate the organ concerned. This has been statistically proved correct and in some cases the diagnosis has been infinitely more accurate than a Western doctor's diagnosis. The sedation would reduce the flow of chi and the stimulation the opposite.

But what is the doctor himself experiencing when he takes this pulse? If he were taking a pulse associated with the liver or kidney he would be testing the chi of those organs and not the strength or regularity of the heartbeat alone. Chi itself is a Yang substance, and each organ of the body and function of the body has its own chi. Some thirty-two types of chi have been defined and when all of them are in harmony we have a very healthy person.

Can we now, without embarrassment, define it as the energy associated with the activity of specific organs and functions of the body? In other words we define it by what it does and not by what it is. If we ask 'What is life?', we cannot expect an answer other than what we experience. We recognise life by its presence and death by its absence.

When T'ai Chi people train they are harmonising the different types of chi in the body. Their experience, as far as it goes, is of all the sources of chi coming together in a better way than they do in the hurly-burly of daily life. If we accept the statements about the beneficial effects of chi from T'ai Chi training on the organs of the body, outlined in the previous chapter then we are heading towards a common agreement about chi. In the West we would say that T'ai Chi training gives us more vitality. Once again we have a word which cannot be defined. But we all know when we have vitality and when not. So, if we need a word to define chi in English we can use the word vitality.

How does T'ai Chi improve our vitality or chi? If we eat sensibly and take regular exercise our vitality improves. This is not the same effect as the effect of T'ai Chi. You will have realised by now that there is more to the art than mechanically putting one foot in front of the other as in jogging or even tennis where more skill is required. In T'ai Chi we are using the attention of the mind, and even of the feeling, combined with the movement of the body. When the brain is disconnected from the spine, the body can still make many movements but one thing it cannot do is maintain an upright or any type of posture apart from lying down. This says something important about the brain and spine relationship. The body, to perform anything but the best known, regularly practised actions, needs to be paid the closest attention. To bring about a change of movement, such as we are doing in our T'ai Chi, needs almost constant close attention, from the mind, from the 'i', in Chinese. This is part and parcel of the experience of chi, of new vitality. If, in addition to this close attention from the mind, there is also a different feeling, let us say from being in a beautiful, early morning setting as in the Chinese tradition, then this feeling also contributes something and the experience of vitality or chi is improved. This tripartite effort of body, feeling and mind, can produce a new experience, characterised by a new, lighter energy. The muscles and tendons and bones are not allowed to move any old which way; they are watched over and brought back into a different rhythm, a different time scale almost, and this in turn feeds back into the mind and feelings giving a constant interplay.

The nearest Western approach to this effect known to the public at large is in Biofeedback. One definition of Biofeedback is 'a process or technique for learning voluntary control over automatically, reflexly regulated body functions'. When Biofeedback is used therapeutically a specific physiological function such as heartbeat, blood pressure or muscle tone is connected to a machine in such a way that the patient can monitor what the level of activity in the function is. Through taking a voluntary part in the monitoring the patient can learn to regulate that function. It has been found for instance in patients with poor circulation in certain parts of the body that it is possible through Biofeedback to improve it. By taking the temperature of the part of the body affected and suggesting to the patient that he raises the temperature by means of his own wish, and displaying to him the temperature on a screen, doctors have found that the patient can indeed bring more blood to the affected part and in time improve the circulation. This is just a simple example and more complex and spectacular results have also been achieved. What Biofeedback indicates is that when you introduce another factor into the situation — the mind and wishes of the patient — and you connect that to a visual aid such as a dial, screen or temperature gauge, and combine this with the knowledge and experience of the doctor or teacher, it is possible to influence the body in quite a different way. In our terms we would say it is possible to influence his chi.

The dial or screen is not the only aid to recovery though. The subjective muscular experience of the man himself can be used. This requires no external aids. In this connection there is someone whose work I think has not been sufficiently made use of and investigated. He is Edmund Jacobson. In the early part of this century, Jacobson, an American doctor, began to study the subject of relaxation and its relationship with curing illness and preventing it. He published many papers and some books on the methods he used and finally presented to the public a layman's guide to his methods. They have much to recommend them.

Briefly, his method involves the ordered tensing and relaxing of different muscles of the body, at a definite speed and for a definite time. Over a long period, and this is important, for it is not a five-minute wonder method, the patient learns to relax very deeply. He is not asleep or hypnotising himself; the method requires prolonged concentration. When he has got to a certain stage in what is called Progressive Relaxation in a still position, he moves on to Differential Relaxation, involving relaxing whilst living one's daily life. Specific parts of the body are relaxed. The 'feedback' comes from the muscles of the body themselves. They are able to relax because they are receiving a different message from usual from the mind. This replaces the usual, unconscious messages which are constantly telling them to tense up.

Jacobson reported excellent results. He is regarded by later followers of the Biofeedback method as a remarkable pioneer in their field. As a man who followed a particular subject so singlemindedly all his life he has my unreserved admiration.

One of the features of his work which is closely connected to our study of T'ai Chi is the relationship between the muscles, the organs of the body, the mind and the emotions and feelings. It is a relationship which G. I. Gurdjieff wrote about in his book *Meetings With Remarkable Men*. Jacobson observed that when a patient thought about a particular place or a particular activity, the muscles of the body associated with that thought were brought into action. The internal organs also responded. When, however, the muscles were intentionally relaxed then the thoughts and physiological activities associated with the muscle activity disappeared or were considerably reduced. The usefulness of such a mechanism in illness is obvious; its ramifications in preventive medicine enormous. But let's look at its ramifications for our T'ai Chi. I am dwelling on Jacobson's work because I think it will make things clearer than trying to define and explain the terminology of Chinese medicine. Once we are clearer and continue to study T'ai Chi and ourselves in practise then perhaps we shall individually come closer to understanding the Chinese writings should we wish to do so.

In fact Jacobson's method provides us with a missing ingredient as T'ai Chi students. When people study T'ai Chi they may obtain the results listed in the first column *when they are training*. But once they stop and go about their business these results tend to evaporate quickly and they get caught up in the hurly-burly of city life.

142

T'ai Chi	Jacobson
Standing still before beginning	Lying down or stopping movement
Moving in a slow, relaxed way	Relaxing specific muscles in movement
Paying attention to movement	Paying attention to specific muscles and movement
Slower and deeper breathing (a result − not forced)	Slower and deeper breathing (a result − not forced)
Few or no thoughts coming into the mind due to concentration on the movement	Few or no thoughts coming into the mind due to concentration on relaxing the muscles
A sense of well being and an increased flow of chi	A sense of calm and well being with increased vitality

Jacobson's method of Differential Relaxation, or something like it, provides us with a bridge between training and life experience. It shows us a direction for finding the peace of the Form in the formless tumult of life.

For instance, Jacobson suggests that when we are sitting at our office or watching television or knitting or riding on the subway we could intentionally relax our legs. This is just a for instance. It is a logical step from this suggestion of his for T'ai Chi students to do the same or something similar from their own art. When at your desk or wherever you are, perhaps you could experiment. Try loosening your knees or relaxing your feet for a few minutes, or just imagine you are doing your T'ai Chi, shift your weight from side to side, and so forth.

Regular application of such methods leads to an increase in appreciation of the value of T'ai Chi and an increase in chi. But what about the 'i', the Chinese 'mind'? T'ai Chi has been called 'Meditation in movement', but it can easily become 'Imagination in movement' if we are not careful. We need a firm foundation. But let's suppose that we are proficient in the Form, relaxed, breathing more easily and can go through the entire sequence of movement without any appreciable break in concentration. It is time to investigate the expression, 'meditation in movement'.

Coming on the heels of Edmund Jacobson, scientists, some more scientific than others, began to take readings from encephalographs showing the brain wave patterns of Zen monks, during, before and after meditation or Zazen sessions. A number of books and papers were published on their findings. There is no consensus on the complete reliability of the findings but certain broad areas of agreement have been reached. One area of agreement is that when a trained Zen monk or other person with similar background carries out what is commonly called 'meditation' the predominant waves emitted by his brain change. According to Tomio Hirai there is a range of five types of brain wave, with gradations between them. I have tried to tabulate his findings very briefly below.

Delta Waves	Occurring in deep sleep	Three per minute	1 Waves at
Theta Waves	Occurring in light sleep	Six per minute	2 each level
Alpha Waves	Calm/stable waking state	Twelve per minute	4 are doubled
Beta Waves	Activity/stress state	Twenty-four per minute	8
Gamma Waves	Fighting pitch	Forty-eight per minute	16

These figures are very broad ones and within each range there are gradations which fall within one particular sphere. For instance, the beta waves cover such activities as steady, attentive work at a new and challenging problem and the beginnings of excitement and stress through overwork and frustration. Hirai, a psychiatrist from the Tokyo Medical School, carried out measurements on numbers of Zen monks and showed that almost immediately after taking up the meditation posture of Zazen a monk would begin to emit waves in the alpha range, indicating calm and stability. After a while he would begin to emit theta waves. Even though these waves are associated in non-meditators with light sleep, the monks were not asleep by ordinary standards. They were still awake.

Although it is a deviation from our subject to some extent, it throws some light on the matter of pupil-teacher relationships, so I shall mention the following. This comes also from Hirai. You may know that there are two main sects of Buddhism in Japan — Rinzai and Soto. The Rinzai sect makes use of what is known as a *koan* to bring insight to the monks. The koan takes the form of a problem which the ordinary reasoning power of the brain, the part which emits Beta waves, cannot possibly solve. For instance, 'What is the sound of one hand clapping?' leaves our minds blank and bewildered. The Rinzai take this koan and work at it, bringing the mind face to face with it again and again during daily chores. At intervals the monks return to the master who has given them the koan and make their reply. Hirai found, during his researches, that when a Zen monk returns to his teacher to present his reply, the teacher never accepts an answer from one who has been trying to use the beta level of the mind, that is, ordinary thinking, to solve his koan. This means, says Hirai, that the teacher is sensitive enough to detect the type of mental activity the monk has been engaged in.

144

The Zen sitting position, Zazen, is very important. The spine, scapula-shoulder region, abdomen, neck and head, all must be correct. When untrained people sit, they sway about a great deal, even though they may believe they are stable and still. Hirai measured the swaying of different people sitting in Zazen and found that the movement of trained monks was minimal. But not even they reached the wooden condition of the fighting cock we spoke of earlier... Zen monks occupy themselves differently when in meditation. There is attention to posture, attention to the breath, counting the breath, and so forth. If you compare this with what we have said about T'ai Chi up to now you will clearly see that a similar possibility is open to us. Both Zen and T'ai Chi can take us deeper into ourselves and away from the surface of life, and closer to a different reality. This applies both in the quiet of a garden and in the busy main street.

In this chapter we have seen how the vitality of chi can be intimately connected to the mind or 'i'. By patiently following the series of steps and suggestions presented in this book, combined with the help of a good teacher, your study of T'ai Chi can take you from experiences pleasurable to profound. In the latter half of the twentieth century this is something to be welcomed.

10

ADDITIONAL RELAXATION METHODS

In addition to the methods more specifically directed towards relaxing for T'ai Chi, there are many others of a less specific nature. It is useful to know some of these just in case you find yourself getting a little stale from time to time and in need of a change.

Although the sequence we are following in these additional exercises begins with the face and works down to the feet there is no hard and fast rule about this at the stage dealt with in this book. Just remember that we are taking relaxation as the key to performing T'ai Chi correctly so no attempt to find new ways will be wasted. Here we go.

We shall alternately tense and relax, tense and relax groups of muscles. Remember to let your breath be as natural as possible. Notice also that when you tense a muscle or set of muscles you can let the rest relax. By cultivating this you can acquire some ability only to use the muscles needed for a particular task.

1. Head and face	raise the muscles of your forehead, hold and relax lower the muscles of your forehead, frown, hold and relax clench your jaw, hold and relax try to move the muscles of the scalp and ears
2. Neck	pull the chin down towards the chest, hold and relax stretch the neck up and then arch it back a little, hold and relax bend the neck to the left side and then the right side, hold and relax
3. Shoulders	lift the shoulders, hold and relax pull the shoulders down, hold and relax push the shoulders forward, hold and relax pull your shoulders back, hold and relax
4. Arms	clench your fist and pull it back towards your forearm, that is, so that the back of your fist approaches the forearm, hold and relax clench the fist and pull it towards your forearm, so that the palm comes nearer the forearm bend your arm, using the biceps muscle, but make sure that your forearm is relaxed, hold and relax push your arm down, straight, at your side, using your triceps, the muscles at the back of your arm, hold and relax

146

5. Back   stretch your back and raise your arms as if you were having a good yawn, hold for a few seconds and relax

6. Abdomen   tense your abdominal muscles, hold and relax

7. Buttocks   contract both buttocks, hold and relax

8. Thighs   tense the muscles at the front of the thighs, hold and relax; then repeat with the muscles at the back of the thighs

9. Lower leg   bend the foot up towards the shin, hold and relax; then bend the foot away from the shin

10. Foot   arch the foot and point toes downward, hold and relax; then bend the toes up

11

REVIEW

In this final section it is worth reviewing the materials we have covered. If you have not made any notes whilst reading then this part may help you focus your thoughts on what you want from T'ai Chi.

1. T'ai Chi is descended from early Taoist practices and so is part of a much wider and deeper world view, which includes man and his relationship with the universe in which he lives. It can be very interesting and rewarding to study this Taoist view and compare it with others. It may also help you to understand T'ai Chi better.

2. You can instead approach it from a different angle. Leaving all Taoist and Chinese associations aside, you can study T'ai Chi from the point of view of healthy exercise.

3. You can take this a step further and make T'ai Chi a starting point for an understanding of yourself, using your body as a firm foundation. The tension and relaxation of the body contains many secrets, not the least of which is their relationship with the thoughts and emotions. By steadily and systematically putting all this together you will find relationships with other teachings about man which will increase your understanding.

4. Remember that relaxation is the key and correct alignment the partner. Minimum effort for maximum result can help you to study relaxation more deeply, which entails slowness at first, and patience.

5. Correct Form follows from this, since it is only when the body is relaxed and aligned that it can assume correct Form.

6. Application of T'ai Chi for self defence is a long-term thing, but there are some immediate advantages in this area such as distancing and alertness to the situation.

7. Though many claims are made on behalf of the health benefits of T'ai Chi, these can hardly be expected to appear if other aspects of one's life such as food, cigarettes and alcohol are not watched to some extent.

8. The psychological benefits which can possibly come from T'ai Chi are many, based once again on relaxation and yielding, opening to another's point of view.

9.   Chi energy for Chinese is empirical — part of experience. It does not need to be demonstrated in a scientific context, any more than a feeling of vitality needs to be demonstrated for us in order to prove its existence.

10.   Other subjects are related to T'ai Chi such as Zen meditation, Biofeedback, Progressive and Differential Relaxation, the Alexander technique, Feldenkrais therapy, and so on.

A last word — if you learn the form and follow the principles, ignore people who tell you that the way you do your T'ai Chi is wrong. If they can demonstrate to you that you are not following the principles then take what they say. But never change because someone says, 'I learned from Master So-and-So and he does it this way.' Stick to what you know. Beauty and aesthetic enjoyment of movement come from correct Form in T'ai Chi. Best of luck.

12 SOME BACKGROUND TO THE ART

Chinese history, perhaps more than the history of any other country, is a veritable patchwork of record and legend. It is difficult to disentangle them and, for our purposes, not even really necessary. One of the most colourful figures in this history is Chang San-feng, an early Taoist immortal whose very existence, let alone period, is open to question by serious scholars.

He was one of a group of eccentrics outside the mainstream of Taoist teachers, and according to one source appeared some time in the fourteenth century AD. The exploits of Chang appealed to the imagination of all classes of society and over the centuries have been repeated and embroidered according to taste. A few things about him are constant, however. He is truly immortal, and continues to appear and disappear according to the dictates of his unique wishes. He attracted the attention of emperors who wished to discover the secret or elixir of life which had given him his immortality. But none gained an audience with him.

Chang called himself the 'Master of Triple Abundance Capable of Endurance and Preserving Harmony'. Like the better known adepts of Tibet, he could sit out in sub-zero temperatures and keep himself quite warm, preserving his life. He needed a lot of energy to do this, not only because of the temperature but because he was also seven feet tall... His appearance resembled that of a crane and tortoise, with huge eyes and a big beard.

He was not born wise, however, and for many years travelled about and studied with Buddhist as well as Taoist teachers. The Wu-tang mountains in Hupeh province are famous because Chang lived there for a time. This strange man is given the credit of founding the art of T'ai Chi. The story is that he learned it in a dream, and proved his efficiency in such a peacefully learned art by killing one hundred bandits who were terrorising a country district. Such a deed places him also in the ranks of the Chinese Knights Errant, another colourful group of figures in Chinese history.

Other accounts of Chang see him as little more than an unkempt tramp or beggar, wandering aimlessly about. Even in this guise he is always cheerful and like another legendary figure, Monkey, always up to tricks. It surely is understandable that the contemporary Taoists did not want their Way cluttered up with such a personage.

Another view of Chang's relationship with T'ai Chi is put forward by William Theodore de Bary, author of *Self and Society in Ming Thought*. The same view is also supported by Dr Tseng Ju-pai, author of *Primordial Pugilism, T'ai Chi Chuan*. They suggest the following.

It is common in Chinese history for a group of people with a common interest to connect themselves with some famous person, in order to boost their prestige, gain respectability and so on. The Shaolin (Sil-lum) Boxers of the Shaolin Temple in Honan took as their adopted patron saint the renowned Bodhidharma (Tamo), who is reputed to have brought the teachings of the Buddha from India to China where he founded the Cha'an school, known after its Japanese migration as Zen. Bodhidharma is always said to have instituted a regime of exercises to toughen up his aspiring monks, and the Shaolin Boxers said that these exercises were the beginnings of their boxing art. De Bary and Tseng claim that the adherents of T'ai Chi, in order to support their cause and art, put forward the redoubtable Chang San-feng as their founder, to try to bring themselves up to par with the Shaolin school.

Whatever the truth it matters little to us now; it is enough to know that our own subject of study was done by the immortals!

A final note on Chang as far as we are concerned. In 1940 a Professor Yoshioka visited the White Cloud temple in Peking and found members of the Chuan-chen sect there, still devoting a shrine to the Immortal Chang. And in 1919 in Shanghai a series of books were published purporting to be the words of Chang, received through a spirit medium who wrote them down in trance.

Several other theories exist about the origins of T'ai Chi but if we want more solid ground we have to come into the nineteenth century and the Yang family. Yang Lu-chan was a nineteenth-century figure who learned the art from the Chen family. The most popular version of this, recently contradicted in an American publication, recounts that Yang was employed as a servant in the Chen household. As he was not a family member he was unable to receive tuition. So, he spied on the Chens as they trained. Such was his innate ability that he was able to pick up the art simply by watching. Finally he was seen practising alone by the head of the family who was so struck by his solitary progress that he admitted him to the classes. Eventually Yang returned to his own territory in Kwang Ping prefecture and defeated many boxing masters who wished to try him out. He came to the attention of a certain Duke Pai in Peking and acted as his bodyguard and mentor in T'ai Chi. Even in Peking, where the best boxers lived, no one could stand up to Yang. One of Yang's sons, Yang-Chien-hou, also a T'ai Chi expert, had two sons: Yang Shao-hou and Yang-Cheng-fu. The name of the latter has come down to the twentieth century as the principle father of modern Yang style T'ai Chi. Among his pupils were Chen Wei-ming and Cheng Man-ch'ing. It is Cheng who is regarded as the main influence in the West on the development of the art.

There are now a number of Chinese and Western pupils of Cheng's who carry his line, including Robert Smith. In Chinese arts the lineage of a man is very important. Who taught him is often more important than what he achieved or knows. Before even thinking of visiting a teacher, a man will ask from whom he learned. Only then may he consider that teacher worth a visit. In recent years the number of T'ai Chi teachers has risen by leaps and bounds. People frequently say to me, 'Oh, so-and-so has started a T'ai Chi class.' I always ask the name of the original teacher. If the answer does not ring a bell then I try to find out who the next teacher in line was and so on. When I strike a name I recognise it helps me to build up an even wider genealogy of instructors and pupils. Sometimes I come across someone who has taught himself from a book. This is not as impossible as it sounds, but I think it is advisable to have some lessons.

Among the styles in existence today are the Sun style, the Fu style, the Wu style, the Chen style and the Yang, plus a few family styles which are 'closed'. This means that at some point a particular teacher took one of the major styles and either changed it on purpose or accidentally or combined it with another style of Chinese boxing or exercise, and continued to call it T'ai Chi. This new style was then kept within a particular family and so was less well known to the outside world. However, in judging the worth of such a style, should you come across one, you have only to bear in mind the principles outlined in this book.

In Great Britain today I know only a few teachers of T'ai Chi Chuan whom I would mention. I say this only because they are the only ones I have met or know about through friends. The first is Rose Li, who teaches in London and is also an exponent of Pakua. The second is Chu, K. H., who is also in London and a disciple of Yang Sau Cheung of San Francisco. The third is John Kells, another London teacher who has devoted most of his adult life to the art. The fourth is Danny Connor of Manchester who now teaches the modern Peking forms. The fifth is Derek Frearson of Leicester who is a pupil of Bow Sim Mark.

The last ten years have seen the appearance of various martial arts from South-East Asia in Europe and in the USA. Some T'ai Chi teachers have appeared from Thailand and South Vietnam. In the USA the best known of these is Mantak Chia in New York. He has made a synthesis of Taoist teachings, including T'ai Chi, which he teaches to Chinese and Western pupils. It is to him that I owe the emphasis placed on the scapula in this book. His Form is short and based strictly on relaxation and correct alignment. I think his influence on the art will be more and more evident with time.

Another teacher in New York is William Chen, a pupil of Cheng. His Form is very soft, yet he is keen on full contact combat and the application of the Form to combat. He is held in high regard.

Madame Bow-sim Mark (Mark, Bow-sim) was born in mainland China and emigrated to the USA a long time ago. She is a Boston-based teacher and is regarded in her country of birth as a leading world expert on both the Forms of T'ai Chi and the weapons of the art. Her current Form is the new, modern form, based on all known T'ai Chi styles and logically enough known as Combined T'ai Chi.

152

I have never seen anyone with her flexibility and smoothness of movement when doing the Form at speed.

In New York there is C. K. Chu who is a strict traditionalist, teaching the Long Form and its application to combat. In San Francisco there is Yang Sau Cheung, teacher of C. K. Chu of London who also emphasises the combat aspects.

We would need another book to go into the many different teachers and Forms in the world. This flowering of interest in the art is indicative that people are looking for something else besides television and hamburgers with which to fill their bodies and minds. It is a hopeful sign.

Bibliography

A selection of books related to this one

T'ai Chi Chuan

Chinese Culture Foundation T'ai Chi Chuan Teacher's Handbook, Kue Lien-ying, California, 1976(?)
Combined T'ai Chi Chuan, Bow-sim Mark, Boston, 1978
Fundamental Exercises of T'ai Chi Chuan, Tang Mong Hun, Singapore, 1965
Fundamentals of T'ai Chi Chuan, Wen Skan Muang, Hong Kong, 1979
Master Cheng's Thirteen Chapters on T'ai Chi Chuan, Cheng Man-ching, Sweet Chi Press, 1982
Practical Use of T'ai Chi Chuan, Yeung (Yang) Sau Chung, Boston, 1977
Primordial Pugilism — T'ai Chi Chuan, Tseng Ju-pai (Chiu Yen), Paul H. Crompton Ltd, 1976
Research into Techniques and Reasoning of T'ai Chi Chuan, Yiu Kwong, (Chinese and English in one volume), Hong Kong, 1978
Simplified T'ai Chi Chuan, Bow-sim Mark, Boston, 1977
T'ai Chi Chuan in Theory and Practice, Kuo Lien-ying, San Francisco, no date
T'ai Chi Chuan, It's Effects and Practical Application, Yearning K. Chen, Hong Kong, 1971
T'ai Chi, Cheng Man-ching and Robert W. Smith, Tuttle, 1967
T'ai Chi Chuan for health and self defence, T. T. Liang, Redwing, 1974
T'ai Chi Chuan, a manual of instruction, Lu Hui-ching, St Martin's Press, 1973
T'ai Chi Touchstones, Compiled by Douglas Wile, Sweet Chi Press, 1983
Tao of T'ai Chi Chuan, Jou Tsung Hwa, Tuttle, 1980

Miscellaneous Subjects

Asian Fighting Arts, Smith & Draeger, Kodansha, 1973

Chinese Boxing, Masters and Methods, Robert W. Smith, Kodansha, 1974

Chinese Medicine, The Web that has no Weaver, Ted J. Kaptchuk, Rider, 1983

Creativity & Taoism, Chang Chung-yuan, Wildwood House, 1973

Hara. the vital centre of man, Karlfried Durckheim, George Allen & Unwin, 1970

I-Ching, or Book of Changes, trans. Richard Wilhelm, Routledge, 1968

In Search of the Miraculous, P. D. Ouspensky, Routledge, 1969

Lao-tze — 'My Words are very easy to understand', Lectures on the Tao Te Ching, Man-jan Cheng (Cheng Man-ching), North Atlantic Books, 1981

Mudra, E. Dale Saunders, Routledge, 1960

Meetings with Remarkable Men, G. I. Gurdjieff, Routledge, 1963

O Ra Te Gama — The Embossed Tea Kettle, Hakuin Zenji, George Allen & Unwin 1961

Self and Society in Ming Thought, Wm. Theodore de Bary, Columbia, 1970

Sources of Chinese Tradition, Vol. 1, Columbia 1960 (A compilation)

Stress and the art of Bio Feed Back, Barbara B. Brown, Harper & Row, 1977

Study of Gurdjieff's Teaching, Kenneth Walker, Jonathan Cape, 1957

Tao Te Ching, trans. Ch'u Ta-Kao, George Allen & Unwin, 1970

To Live Within, Lizelle Reymond, George Allen & Unwin, 1972

You Must Relax, Edmund Jacobson, Unwin Paperbacks, 1980

(The) Way and its Power, Arthur Waley, Unwin Paperbacks, 1968

Zen and Japanese Culture, D. T. Suzuki, Princeton, 1973

Zen and the Mind, Tomio Hirai, Japan Publications, 1978

Zen Flesh, Zen Bones, Paul Reps, Penguin Books, 1957

(The) Zen Life, Sato & Kuzunishi, Weatherhill, 1977

Zen Meditation Therapy, Tomio Hirai, Japan Publications, 1975

Zen Mind, Beginners Mind, Shunryu Suzuki, Weatherhill, 1979

(A First) Zen Reader, Trevor Leggett, Tuttle, 1971

Zen Training, Katsuki Sekida, Weatherhill, 1977

INDEX

Alexander Technique   1

'Beginning'   42
'Bend Bow'   86
Biofeedback   141
Bodhidharma   151
Book of Changes   104
brain waves   144
breathing   31
'Brush Left Knee'   57

Chang San-feng   150
Chang Siew-pang   134
Chen style   151
Chen Wei-ming   151
Chen, William   152
Chen, Yearning K.   133
Cheng, Man-ch'ing   131
ch'i   138
Chia, Mantak   152
Chu, C. K.   152
Chu, K. H.   153
Connor, Danny   152
'Cross Hands'   62

diagnosis   140
'Diagonal Flying Posture'   70
Differential Relaxation   143
Double Push Hands   97

'Embrace Tiger'   64

'Fair Lady'   79
fighting cock   27
Five Excellences   127
Frearson, Derek   152
Fu style   152
Fundamental Substances   140
fundamentals   2

Geddes, Gerda   1
'Golden Cockerel'   73
Gurdjieff, G. I.   32

health   131
'Holding the Ball'   44
hyung   36

'i'   145

Jacobson, Edmund   142
Jou, Tsung-hwa   131
Judo   91

kata   36
Kells, John   152
koan   144

Lee, Douglas   133
Leggett, Trevor   123
Li, Rose   152
Liang, T. T.   133
Lien, Ying-kuo   89
'Lifting Hands'   55
Liu, Hui-ching   33

Maisel, Edward   32
Mark, Bow-sim   134
meridians   139
Monkey posture   29
music   126

oriental medicine   138

'Play Guitar'   58
'Preparation'   41
'Press'   48
Progressive Relaxation   142
pulse   140
'Punch Under Elbow'   66
'Push'   50
Pushing Hands   90

Qu, Mian-yu   134

relationship   130
relaxation   18, 146
'Ride Tiger'   82
Rinzai Zen   144
'Rollback'   46

scapula   25
secrets   2,5
Sekida, Katsuki   34

self defence   106
'Separate Left Foot'   76
'Separate Right Foot'   75
Shaolin   151
shift weight   36-39
'Single Whip'   52
'Single Whip Squatting'   73
'Shoulder Stroke'   55
Smith, Robert W.   138, 151
Soto Zen   144
'Step Back – Monkey'   68
'Step Forward – Punch'   58
'Step – Seven Stars'   82
'Strike with Heel'   76
Supreme Ultimate   139
symmetry   128

Taijiquan, benefits   134
Tang, Mun-hon   134
Tao   31
Taoist   150
Tseng, Ju-Pai   133
Tung, Mao-tse   90

van Briessen   124
Vitality (& Ch'i)   140

Waley, Arthur   90
'Ward Off Left'   44
'Ward Off Right'   46
'Waving Hands in Clouds'   71
'Withdraw and Push'   50
Wu style   12
Wu-tang mountains   150

Yang, Cheng-fu   151
Yang, Chien-fou   151
Yang family   151
Yang, Lu-chan   151
Yang, Ming-shih   133
Yang, Sau-cheung   153
Yang, Saho-hou   151
Yin-Yang   139
Yoga   130

zazen   145
Zen calligraphy   123